Love Yourself

It All Begins with You

Jamai Wray

Love Yourself: It All Begins with You. Copyright 2022 by Jamai Wray. All rights reserved. No part of this publication may be reproduced, distributed, or transmitte d in any form or by any means, including photocopying, recording, or other electronic or mechanical methods, without the prior writte n permission of the publisher, except in the case of brief quotations embodied in critical reviews and certain other noncommercial uses permitted by copyright law.

For permission requests, write to the publisher, addressed "Attention: Permissions Coordinator," 15606 107th Avenue, Suite #101, Jamaica, NY 11433. M Wray Publishing books may be purchased for educational, business or sales promotional use. For information, please email the Sales Department at mwrayent@gmail.com.

Printed in the U. S. A.

First Printing, June 2022.

Library of Congress Cataloging-in-Publication Data has been applied for.

ISBN: 978-1-7370519-0-9

For my two kids,

Janai-Monet and Jamai Amir Wray,

Daddy's legacy.

"Every man knows that his highest purpose in life cannot be reduced to any relationship. If a man prioritizes his relationship over his highest purpose, he weakens himself, disservices the universe, and cheats his woman of an authentic man who can offer her his full, undivided presence."

— David Deida

Contents

Preface 1
Introduction 3
What are Universal Laws? 6
The F.I.G. Tree 9

Part 1 The Root: Understanding Yourself 11

Where did you learn love? 13
Hurt people, hurt people 22
It is time to move on 25
The F.I.G Tree 27
The F.I.G Tree 28
Universal Laws 29

Part 2 The Trunk: Loving Yourself 39

The beginning, the evolution 41
It all begins with you 48
Mentorship 67

Get your shit together first 74
Love Yourself like you would love your significant other 77
Self-awareness and the Ego 98
Confidence: You must want something.......................................102
What glitters is not always gold..104
Self-preservation 108
Sell the experience 110
Elevator Pitch...116
The Power of Self-talk and Visualization....................................119
What is fear?...131
Keep dreaming, even if it breaks your heart 134
The F.I.G Tree 137
The F.I.G Tree 138
Universal Laws...140

Part 3 The Branches: Your Awakening 153

Paying attention to the signs 155
The F.I.G Tree 165
Universal laws 166

Part 4 The leaves: Loving Again 169

Loving Again, but first... 171
Principles of love 173
Chemistry and Compatibility 175
The F.I.G Tree 180
The F.I.G Tree 182
Universal Laws 185
Recap and Clarity 186
Acknowledgements 193
About the Author 195
Also by Jamai Wray 196
Selected Bibliography 197

Preface

This book was not intended to be my next project. I wanted to truthfully finish writing my first novel. I mean, it is halfway complete, but for some reason, lately, I haven't been gravitating to it cosmically. So I thought it was the best move as a company and personally as an artist, to switch up genres and show range, but like love, life always has a different plan for you than your own.

It was clear to me that I was not done sharing my story. I was not done sharing my truth and the truth we all share as human beings experiencing life in this physical world. It is experiences that give this book breath and it is my growth that pumps the blood to its heart. This book is alive because we are alive. We are here to serve each other - so it was a no-brainer to once again, be at service.

My aim in life has always been to be the person I wish I had growing up. This book shows you the power of your story. The power of your words and thoughts. The power in your actions and beliefs. The power of decision making and the impact your decisions will have on the older you.

I stress all the time to people that ten years goes by in a blink of an eye. If you don't care enough to respect yourself now, then at least respect your ten-years–from-now self. Because if he or she knew you could do better and didn't do better, he or she is going

LOVE YOURSELF

to be mad at you. You are going to be upset at the lack of risk, the lack of discipline, and the refusal to want to be the best version of yourself. You're going to be mad at you.

In my opinion, there is no better motivation than the success story of someone who turned everything completely around and became a better version of themselves. Creating a routine is important to give you structure so you can begin to build the discipline that's necessary to be consistent. Passion must come from you to fuel the ambition to want to succeed. All you have to do is take it one day at a time. Never rush. Never force. Always be authentic. And whatever you end up doing will be from the consistent effort you put in every day. Most importantly, it will show up in how you treat others.

Introduction

Have you ever scrolled down your Facebook page and wondered if you were wasting all your genius about life, love, and philosophy by giving quotes and stories freely to the world? Have you ever thought or has anyone suggested that if structured properly, all your profound quotes and stories would make a fantastic book? Have you ever thought about the hidden message within your story and how it would help others? Yes, no, maybe? Great. Because that is exactly the origin and inspiration behind this book.

A friend of mine did just that. She suggested that I speak about all that I had accomplished after my break-up. She believed that my story could save lives and change the minds of a generation. Because of her encouragement and influence, I would like to present to you *Loving Yourself: It All Begins with You.*

Observing humans (and I do not know why that sounds like I am some superior sapien or something) has shown me that we are dumb. We are easily manipulated. We do not question anything and we are mostly naïve. We pay to live on an Earth that grows all we need for free while we work five jobs to still be in debt. Walking outside costs a hundred dollars and love is impossible to find because everyone is weird, insecure, fake, egomaniacal, negative, angry, prideful, sociopaths, or have daddy and mommy issues.

The system that runs this world could care less about us and society dysfunction has created these monsters. The system is set up to keep us focused on everything that takes away our power. To disable our potential and feed us propaganda like we are cattle, programming our kids, grandkids, and great grandkids so we lose all sovereignty and power over our own lives and future. Look at our schools, the history being taught is false. The structure is outdated, it teaches us how to work and feed the system, but not how to create and cultivate for ourselves.

We live in a system that keeps us stagnant for most of our lives, enslaving our minds through programming that prevents us from tapping into our authenticity. This will take a lifetime to rectify. We spend most of our lives in love with the wrong things and/or people making retirement a baby shower for death, which is sad, because it is not supposed to be that way.

We have been conditioned to not go against the norm and to accept things as is, even when it does not make sense. We have been conditioned to be self-destructive. With all that has been done to keep us from elevating to our true position among the stars and truly being happy, it makes sense why there is so much unhappiness in our lives, our jobs, and relationships.

We do not know what the hell we are doing because we are being misled.

Our mental health as a people has been poisoned and our lives do not matter to whoever controls it all. Our priorities are not in order. Therefore, we put things like relationships before purpose. We prioritize everything outside of ourselves to win, when winning can only come from working on our inner selves.

I authored this book for people who are putting or who have put relationships before their purpose, who are victims of this societal disorder. This book is for those distracted by loving the right things at the wrong time. This book is for those who are not aware that they expect someone else to pay the tab for their happiness. This book is for couples in relationships trying to understand whether to move forward or not, and what red flags to avoid.

I hope to teach you how to reevaluate standards and boundaries or just call it quits and end it. For my single man or woman who has not experienced love yet, or the ones looking to love again, this book is a guide to understanding why you make the decisions you make and how your past trauma(s) can dictate the void in your life and dysfunction in your relationship.

Whether you are experiencing it now, have experienced it before, or want to prevent having this experience in your future, I am here to share my experiences on where I learned love and how I compromised my happiness in the name of it.

What are Universal Laws?

The Universal Laws are principles that create balance and harmony within all living things. These laws have always existed. It is why everything in the cosmos exists. It is the formula of life. The most well-known law is the Law of Attraction, which highlights giving and receiving based on the energy level you vibrate at. It is only one of the many laws that I will be using throughout this book.

When you understand that the elements that exist within you are the same elements and formula of creation, you understand that we all originate from the same life force. We are pieces of God and our creator is simply looking at itself through different eyes. The cosmos and everything in it are simply an expression. Pieces of the whole. Which means within us we have a tremendous power to create. Not at the scale of planets and galaxies, but for what we can create here on Earth as humans.

Because we are controlled by a religion and powers that take the power from us, we become optimistic or hopeful. We have lost our way and are inadvertently living in a false reality of purpose.

The best one can do at this point is to understand their own trauma, to become a better person for themselves and for their loved ones, to pass on one's experiences and wisdom, and to open the eyes of their fellow man. To make living through this controlled state of being as joyous as possible.

Understanding the universal laws is understanding yourself. This is not a knock against religion or its commandments. Yes, thou shall not kill and murder, and thou shall not steal, but these laws do not help with how to deal with a mother who told her son she should have flushed him down the toilet, nor does it help the young man whose father was not there. It also does not help with mental health issues or address the trauma and drama we as a people deal with in our everyday lives.

These laws do not address how we are victims of systematic control. With any law, if you do not follow it, you will suffer the consequences of your actions and/or inactions. My job is to show you that once you understand and apply these laws you will discover the root of your fears, insecurities, and guilt. You will no longer be controlled or held hostage by the negative opinions of others and yourself. You will be able to get out of your own way. Unless you understand this, you will always be in a mess you need to clean up. Nothing goes away because we hope it does. For the laws to work in your favor and for you to truly gain control over your life, you must be able to ask and answer the toughest questions.

What are you afraid of? Has failure killed your drive? Are you scared of rejection? Do you believe in yourself? Why don't you believe in yourself? What disappoints you most about yourself? Who do you blame for why you are where you are in your life right now? Why do you keep attracting the same poisonous relationships? What are you doing wrong and why? Why are you scared to take the steps needed to achieve your goals when you know you have what it takes? Why are you worried so much about other people's opinions?

The Universal Laws are not something man created. Like I mentioned earlier, these laws of nature have always existed. It was not until man was gifted language that we were able to articulate what we saw in nature and see how these same processes apply to our own lives. I will show you what happens when you go against the universal laws with personal situations and the consequences of my actions. I will show you how I worked against these laws and how I used them to work for me to enhance and advance my personal and professional life.

    Below is a F.I.G. tree. Its strongest branches are Fear, Insecurities, and Guilt. For here on out, I will give you the practical guide on removing this F.I.G. tree from your garden and plant the seeds of loving yourself by way of the laws of nature. I want to help you see that you are your own God and recognize how these universal laws can help you create the happiness we all seek.

THE F.I.G. TREE

Fear **I**nsecurities **G**uilt

The reason I encourage you to write in this book is because writing connects the cerebral to the palpable and tangible. Writing it sends it off into the Universe. With positive and focused intent, truth, and action behind it, the force becomes that much stronger, turning potential and desires into reality.

Your greatest defeat is not following through.

Part 1

The Root: Understanding Yourself

When you do not get to the root of a problem, you cannot solve it in any meaningful manner. People like to look at the surface, get all emotional and react, doing things that make them feel better in the short term but do nothing for them in the long term. This must be the power and the direction of your mind whenever you encounter a problem—to bore deeper and deeper until you get at something basic and at the root. Never be satisfied with what presents itself to your eyes. See what underlies it all, absorb it, and then dig deeper. Always question why this event has happened, what the motives of the various actors are, who really is in control, who benefits from this action. You may never get to the actual root, but the process of digging will bring you closer. And operating in this way will help develop your mind into a powerful analytical instrument.

– Robert Greene/50 CENT

Where did you learn love?

The first question you must ask yourself regarding love is, where did you learn love? If you are going to get the full understanding and wisdom of love, you must get to the root. To define your very existence and purpose will be essential to learning where you learned love from and how it affects you in your life and in your relationships.

So, where did you learn love? Take all the time you need and just think about it. Where did you learn, love? If you are like most of us, you learned it at home. Did you have both parents or you grew up in a single parent home? Were you raised by the streets? Your grandparents maybe? Your father? Ask yourself, who shaped love for you? Who and what is responsible for how you love now?

Have you ever taken the time to think about the root of what molded you to be who you are? Because you did not just wake-up one morning and become shitty at relationships. (Not just with other people either, but with yourself too.) You did not just wake-up and become your own worst enemy. You were made this way.

You have practiced fear, self-doubt, poor eating habits, and laziness all your life. All this time you have been practicing everything but how to absolutely love yourself. Therefore you are great at it, yet this is exactly why you are not happy. As an adult,

LOVE YOURSELF

for an exceptionally long time, I could not have cared less about love. This attitude came from watching my mother because she made me feel unloved.

She just couldn't care less about love. She provided the basics: food, shelter, and clothing. She was great at doing homework, we could not leave that table until we got it right no matter the hour. But when it came to showing love and affection, she did not know how. She did not know how to show the emotion of love.

Now growing up was not that bad. My neighborhood in the late 80s and early 90s provided a lot of adventure. With two siblings and a crew of friends all around the same age, we would spend hours building clubhouses, go-karts, ramps, playing in empty lots with old bulldozers, empty warehouses, and jumping train tracks from roof-to-roof. The fascination of BB guns and riding our bikes trying to get lost was life well spent every day of the summer.

My mother and I had a tough relationship for a long time at one point. I remember feeling like she wished she had never had us. Like we messed up her groove or something. After the death of my father, she put her needs and her life before her kids and family. Now, this is not to bash her, nor am I upset. I have dealt with this. We have been on good terms for years and I concluded that she did the best job she knew how, based on WHAT she knew and how she was raised. But I suffered a great deal of emotional trauma and for a long time, I felt like she did not care about me.

I would always hear how much of a selfish motherfucker I was for focusing so much on what I wanted to do with my life. I took it personally for an exceptionally long time. I am sure other family members and friends felt the same about me, but my mother was animated and vocal about it.

I felt like she wanted me to fail, wanted to keep the genius in me down. I felt at times that she was jealous of me. Do you know what that can do to a young child's confidence and self esteem? Emotional and verbal abuse is like cancer stifling an underdeveloped mind. What if I believed it? What if I was not immune to the poison? What if I was not able to use it as fuel? What if it has haunted and hurt me, how would I know? Where would it show in my life?

I lived an exceptionally large part of my life wanting to prove I was who I said I was. To show that I am the man I say I am. Maybe my mom just wanted the best for me. Maybe she thought I was a psycho and wanted to save me from myself. After all, she is from a different era with a different mindset. But there are some things she claimed we never paid attention to: her strength and independence.

There are a lot of things I have given her more credit for over the years once I finally looked at what I had compared to what my life could have been. She always preached how much she did not need a man or need to depend on anyone. The greatest advice she gave us, that went into one ear and out the other, is, "If you can't take care of yourself and your partner were to 'fall off' and vice versa, then the two of you do not need to be together."

It infuriated my mother that her sons "didn't think like their mama." Or "didn't use the brain God gave us" when it came to us picking women. I watched my mother's relationship with my stepfather and how she took the lead. Even though she was married, she was the dominant masculine one. That is how she loved, by proving she did not need you for anything. No matter who you were to her. She was quiet. She never spoke of her past. Never schooled us about the game of life.

I recall her telling us that she was not going to leave us anything in her will because she did not want us riding around in Bentleys and "living better than her," and that she was going to leave everything to my cousin. He had a civil service job like her. So, to her, he was better than us because they both had city jobs and we, her kids, did not, or at least do something that she would respect.

But I had to ask myself, why is she like this? Why does she and her siblings constantly fight over who got their mother the most expensive gift? Why is she throwing her MTA job, her money, and the fact that she takes care of their parents in her brother and sister's faces? I had to go to her root. Her childhood. And I figured it out. See, she was the baby. Her older brother and sister were extremely popular. My Aunt had a lot of friends, very bubbly personality, smart, gift of gab; she was awesome. Her brother, my uncle, was also extremely popular. My mother, not so much. She felt like her siblings got better clothes and more attention than she did. This created jealousy. She grew up feeling like she had to earn the love that others got for free.

She looked up to her brother, but he was never around. He was always running the streets. The only man in her life was not there for her. I can relate to that because my sister once articulated that she felt that about me. My mother felt that all her life she had lived in the shadows of her brother and sister. I have no doubt in my mind that her siblings made my mother feel inadequate and picked on her at some point.

Now fast forward to the future, they are now adults, but the tables have turned. My mother met the right guy, got the house, and the city job. Both her siblings lived with her at one point. It almost seems like she could not wait for this day to come. To be on top. To be large and in charge. To have power and control—or to prove that they need her and not the other way around. Ironically, I am the same way. I want to prove I am who my mother said I wasn't. I want to throw in her face my success and be large and in charge just like she once did to her siblings. For her making me feel the same way they used to make her feel. It is the cycle of trauma repeating itself.

I want you to do me a favor and answer these questions on the next page. (**1**) Think back to the very first time you fell in love as an adult. Your first real adult relationship. Did how this person love you resemble how you were loved growing up? (**2**) If not, write down how the love you received from this person differed from the love you received at home. (**3**) If yes, how is the love you received from your partner the same as what you received at home? (**4**) What are some of the emotional and verbal abuse you received in your relationship(s) that you also received at home? Take your time and really think about this. There is no rush and please be honest.

LOVE YOURSELF

1. Think back to the very first time you fell in love as an adult. Your first real adult relationship. Did how this person love you resemble how you were loved at home?

___

2. If not, write down how the love you received from this person differed from the love you received at home.

___

3. If yes, how is the love you received from your partner the same as what you received at home?

_____
_____
_____
_____
_____
_____

4. What are some of the emotional and verbal abuse you received in your relationship(s) that you also received at home?

_____
_____
_____
_____
_____
_____
_____

When I fell in love for the first time it was like looking in the mirror. I saw a lot of myself in her. She had an answer for everything, your classic know-it-all. The person who must always have the last word. Listens to reply. I knew her better than she knew herself. Or at least I thought so. Because of this assumption and the fact that she reminded me so much of myself, I mistook pity for understanding and understanding for love. Letting negative behavior go unscathed.

She was embarrassed of me. I had to lie about my age. I lied and disowned my own kids just to make her happy with a fantasy because I was mad at everything, everyone, and myself. Talk about trauma. She hated that I knew more than her, that I had a great depth of knowledge and experience. It felt at times she was jealous of me. As if I made her insecure or intimidated. As if I reminded her of what she was not.

One of the things I should have listened mostly to from my mother was when she said to never give your girl ammunition to fire back at you. Everything should be on a need-to-know basis. Of course, I did not listen. Whenever we would get into arguments, she would bring up how unaccomplished I was at my age and how at my age I am supposed to have this and how she has friends younger than me with more. She would mention the very pain I have been trying to heal from for most of my life.

SHE. WAS. EXACTLY. LIKE. MY. MOTHER. She was quiet. Kept her emotions to herself. It was like we were competing all the time. I did not see any of this until after our relationship was done, but think about it - if my girl wants me to lie about who I am, disown my past, and lie about my kids, is she really in love with who I am or the person she wishes I was?

What does this say about me if I am willing to lie about my age, my kids, and my past? It says I wanted to be who she wished I was.

I withheld my truth to protect her image and most importantly because I did not like myself either.

I was reading this piece from my first book called "I'm an Addict" where I described my addiction to "Knowledge and Wisdom" and "More & Better." I thought about my relationship and the addictive and controlling qualities it possessed and immediately realized if this were a drug deal, I would be the addict and she would be the supplier. The one who needs less is the one in control of the relationship. I learned that from my mother. Because of my ex's youth and ambition and because she did not have any kids or any real responsibility to restrict her or her goals, I saw her better than myself.

It was all about her, and this is what she wanted. She did not need me and because she did not have any baggage, she had many options. Deep down I thought I could not do better. There were other signs I ignored, but we will talk about that later. The point is, I did not know myself enough to love myself and I avoided loving myself. I attracted and fell in love with the same low frequency that vibrated in my childhood home. When you do not love yourself or understand that all your relationships are a product of who you are and how you treat yourself, you will continue to attract fear, insecurity, and guilt and bleed on people who did not cut you.

Hurt people, hurt people

Whatever disharmony you have in your relationship is the same disharmony that was in your home. How your mother loved your father is how you will love your boyfriend. How your mother loved you is how you will expect your girlfriend to love you. How your father loved you is exactly how your boyfriend will love you and how your father loved your mother is how you will love your girlfriend. The absence of the masculine or feminine essence in a household does not mean you do not learn love. It just means that you learn about it from a single perspective/source. Everything has a beginning and reason for its existence. For me, comprehending the root of my troubles clarified why I expected my ex-girlfriend to pay the tab for my happiness.

I was looking for acceptance from her the same way I was looking for it from my mother. Because I was raised in a home where I was told I was not the person I claimed to be and that my head was too far in the clouds chasing a person I do not have the talent to be, that constant beat down of my confidence created a person who always felt they had to prove themself to be loved.

Unfortunately, my ex-girlfriend and I did not make it. In my immaturity and lack of self-control, I slept with the mother of my kids to selfishly fulfill my emotional needs and justify my actions by blaming her lack of support. Although I am human, this is not an excuse. We cheat to get what we are not getting and that is a fact in my book.

It is because of this self-destructive behavior that what I thought would be forever…ended. Our relationship is over and I take full responsibility. You cannot blame anyone else for you not loving yourself, especially when you know enough to do better.

My ex-girlfriend and I were no longer together but still shared an apartment when I began to entertain another woman. I always heard that the best way to get over an ex is to get with someone new. So instead of healing, focusing on and learning how to love myself, I started talking to this young lady, who coincidentally, was going through a comparable situation to me. We became each other's cushion. We vibrated at the same frequency, which is why we were attracted to each other in the first place. I would talk to her about my poison and she would talk to me about hers. We were each other's alcohol, each other's escape. I realize now that hooking up immediately following my breakup only served as a distraction to mask the pain.

Our need to escape reality was the intoxication that fooled us to believe we had found sobriety in each other. But it was nothing but a reflection of the mess we were personally in. If you are dating someone, my solution for you is to try and find out how that person was raised. A lot of people were not raised with proper love. Some were raised to survive, at times under abusive conditions. Do not let success and good looks fool you. You will find that a lot of successful people are damaged inside because of their past and you will not realize how damaged they are until you try to love them.

There are going to be nights you want to hold someone and be held. Days you wished he or she sat on the other side of the table. Moments you see couples and are reminded of what was. Love is the greatest gift you should want from life, but I urge you to embrace this journey and learn why you are the way you are.

    A clear sign that you do not love yourself is when you put up with whatever anyone throws your way, even when you know it is wrong, even when it hurts. Being happy is a very personal thing and does not involve anyone but you. The only reason you suck at giving love to others is because you suck at giving love to yourself. Everything reflects how you deal with and treat yourself, which is why hurt people, hurt people. And most times they are unaware of why they are the way they are or how to fix it.

It is time to move on

It is one thing to get to the root of why you are the way you are and an entirely different thing to honestly believe it does not define you. I know it hurts; I know it is hard to believe in yourself after being told what you cannot do. I know it is hard to detach yourself from the pain and depression that comes with it. I know it is hard to forgive those who hurt you when your life reflects the decisions *they* made. It could be hard to even forgive yourself. But it is time to move on. It is time to move past the fear, insecurities, and guilt that is holding you back from being who you truly are. I am 39 years old and I am tired of talking about this shit.

I am tired of wallowing in my sorrows. I am tired of blaming my mother and society. I am tired of being the victim. As much as I was screwed out of opportunities to be great because of my mother's decisions, if I do not forgive her for my sake, I will never heal. I will never be happy and my demise will be of my own doing and no one else's.

At some point in your life no one will want to hear the excuses. They may understand and pity you, but it is your life and you must take control of it and be accountable for it. Forgiveness and understanding are the greatest acts of love. It took me an exceptionally long time to forgive my mother as well as myself for a lot of things.

LOVE YOURSELF

Understanding the root of why I allowed the things I did helped take away the guilt. This put me in a mental space to begin to learn how to love myself. On the next page is the F.I.G tree, followed by questions I had to answer with complete honesty to be able to move forward. I urge you to do the same on the following page. I will never ask you for something I am not willing to give myself. We all deal with fear, insecurity, and guilt. Here is my truth.

THE F.I.G TREE

What do you *fear*?
JAMAI: I fear that I will waste my gifts and become another statistic. That my talents will never evolve into success.

What are you *insecure* about?
JAMAI: That at 39 years old I have no results to prove my claim that I am smart and talented.

What do you feel *guilty* about?
JAMAI: I feel guilty for disowning my own flesh and blood and dealing with a woman who would allow me to do it.

THE F.I.G TREE

What do you *Fear*?

_____
_____
_____

What are you *Insecure* about?

_____
_____
_____

What do you feel *Guilty* about?

_____
_____
_____

Universal Laws

How to understand and improve who you are through …

- The Law of Belief,
- The Law of Detachment, and The Law of Forgiveness

UNIVERSAL LAW OF BELIEF

The universal law of belief states that we do not believe what we see, we rather see what we have already decided to believe. This universal law is a foundational law of life. Without wholeheartedly believing that something can become a part of your reality, it consequently will always remain out of your reach — no matter how desperately you may want it. Unfortunately, life does not give us what we want but rather what we intend with feeling — whether that intention lies at a conscious or unconscious level of awareness.

— Adam Sicinski

Once my talent surfaced, I began having visions of being great. The more my talent grew, the greater were the achievements I saw myself accomplishing. I talked so much shit about how great I was going to be that it began to annoy people. And those who could not see what I saw made me feel like I was delusional. I had no idea what universal laws were at this time, so I had nothing to reference. I did not have anybody I looked up to, so my inspiration came from only what many would say was my arrogance. Influenced by religion, I was led to believe that I did not control my destiny but that God has a plan for all of us and His plan for me was not what I wanted it to be.

It wasn't until I came across the book, *Entrepreneur's in Profile—How 20 of the World's Greatest Entrepreneurs Built Their Businesses… and How You Can Too,* that I understood who I was. I saw myself in their stories. I was 21 years old and all over the place. I just started recording music and I remember the engineer not taking my session seriously. He was dozing off and very uninterested. I left there thinking maybe my mother was right, which justified her behaviors and other actions.

Entrepreneurs in Profile helped me understand who I was and showed me things that came from believing in yourself. Everyone's story from Berry Gordy, Spike Lee, Oprah, Bill Gates, Reginald Lewis, and many more, all had the same consistency. I had the very same routine and structure. This made me feel like I was no different from them. This is what gave me confidence. Even later when I came across Tyler Perry's story, it just reinforced what I could not explain, which is that I am great. And if I keep pushing and keep believing, success is inevitable.

I always see people get mad, like I once did, at friends and family for never supporting them and the fact that it is always strangers who show the most support. But your dream is your dream. You cannot expect anyone to see it the way you do. You cannot expect anyone to support you if they do not even support themselves. Most people need to see tangible evidence to believe and that is okay, but for us, we believe so much more because we see it in our heads.

Do not lose sight of that vision because you think you are not where you should be. No, you are exactly where you need to be. If you believe the power to control what you want is the responsibility of someone or something else and not within yourself, you will remain exactly where you are. Without believing and doing the work there will be no manifestation of the reality you want. Believing in any higher power more than yourself just as gravely does a disservice to the energy you need to create your reality.

How God works is simple, with focused thought (vibration), intent, and action (energy you release), you create a frequency that aligns people, circumstances, and resources to bring you what you desire. Or in cliché terms, when you hear people say, God continues to bless me. Blessings come by actions on your beliefs. You cannot use prayer to replace laziness.

If you allow the energy of doubt to overpower the belief in yourself, if you believe that person or persons who made you feel worthless, like you would never be anything, then the energy of your potentiality decreases and your talents will never evolve into success.

I was afraid that I had become one of the many people who will never make their dreams come true, so my belief had to be stronger. When you become older and are still dragging your feet to the finish line, what was once used as fuel to motivate you - all the "you are not who you say you are" and other verbal abuse - I now realize were seeds of doubt disguised as courage. So like then, today I must BELIEVE even more because I am not that 17-year-old being told by his mother what he ain't and using it as fuel to prove her wrong. No, I am 39 years old and know I have so much more to prove. What was once fuel now must be turned over to clean renewable energy if I am going to survive.

You will always manifest what you feel, not what you think, and you feel it because you believe it. Even when the odds are against you, trust the process and NEVER STOP BELIEVING IN YOUR CREATIVE ABILITY.

UNIVERSAL LAW OF DETACHMENT

The universal law of detachment says that to acquire anything in the physical universe, you must relinquish your attachment to it. This does not mean you give up the intention to create your desire. You do not give up the intention, and you do not give up the desire. You give up your attachment to the result.

– Deepak Chopra

A huge part of loving yourself and moving forward in life is detaching yourself from the pain of your past and focusing on what you can control today. Again, the energy of holding onto the past just recreates it and you'll find yourself constantly talking about it with your siblings, close friends, or even yourself. It is not about revenge. It is not about the money, the house, or cars. It is not about proving your competence and capabilities. It is not about showing the non-supporters that you were right and how great you always knew you were. No. Get that out of your head. For so long my intent was focused on these things. My desire was to prove to everyone that they were wrong about me.

It was not even about proving it to myself. All my energy and attachments were rooted in fears, insecurities, and material consumption, which is why professionally and personally I was lost and confused and making bad decisions. I was holding on to so much anger that it blocked my ability to love and be loved.

In addition, my intent was not based in love or in the service of others, but a selfish egotistical pursuit to cause pain. Based on the law of detachment I had to relinquish my attachment to the result, which would have been the look on their faces when I proved them wrong. In this case, even my intent had to change because my intent was to be condescending and deprecative, which is sad. I had to remove all the anger, blame, and negative intent behind what I called fuel—the need to prove myself.

The first thing I had to do was love the person I am. To accept me as I am. To understand that not everyone is going to understand me as I am and that is okay. To know that my past does not define me. Once you accept who you are, be grateful for being the one out of four hundred trillion or more to be brought from the darkness of the womb into the light of life.

When you love the color you are, the size you are, the culture you represent, how outspoken you are, and have comfort being you because there is nothing to prove, the guilt that created the fear of inadequacy is no longer there. When you are not mad at how you turned out, it takes away the blame you put on yourself and others.

Ultimately achieving fearlessness transforms loving yourself into being able to forgive others. I am no longer ashamed of decisions I have made because I am not defined by my mistakes, but instead by what I have done to make it better. Self-hate is the deadliest form of cancer. I realized there were certain things I had learned through my struggle that could not have come from a book nor from school.

There is a certain value of knowledge that experience gives you that you cannot get without struggle, which is why I really recommend embracing risk. Going through life safe and calculated will not show you who you are. All I have acquired from life I consider to be priceless. My great qualities come from decisions I have made and those made for me, and though in those moments it was scary, lonely, and unclear where I would end up in life, the wisdom I obtained is priceless.

So what is the first thing I had to fix once I accepted who I was? My relationship with my mother. This is the source of it all for me. But to forgive, you must first understand. Searching for the root of my mother's behavior gave me what I needed to start this process. What I acquired was the understanding I needed. Just like what's discussed in Tom Burrell's book, *Brainwashed, When You Search for the Root of Why People are The Way They Are, You Learn Why the Apple Came Out the Way It Did*, seeing and coming to terms with how alike my mother and I were, helped me understand. Even if her intent was malice and all my claims are true, what justice does it serve me, my purpose, or my family, if love isn't the driving force behind my energy? What becomes of my future if I cannot let go of my past? Plus, she is my mother, the only one I have and will ever have.

There was a time when it was just the two of us, when I made her the happiest person in the world just by smiling. To be mad at her and blame her for how my life turned out could not continue if I wanted peace. I had to forgive. For me to forgive, I had to detach myself from what drove the pursuit of my dream. I had to change my intent.

To change my intent, I had to believe that my failures are still my accomplishments because I am still alive. I am still breathing. And every day above the ground is an opportunity to become the best version of myself. Life is too short to hold a grudge against the person who gave you your life, or anyone for that matter. Always be the bigger person and let love and the service of others be your motivation...and what fuels your intent.

JAMAI WRAY

LAW OF FORGIVENESS

Why is there a need to forgive? The lack of forgiveness creates grief, despair, resentment, and anger within your heart and mind. It skews your perception of what is true, leads you to make assumptions and decisions based on false parameters, and generates unhappiness and lack of fulfillment within your life. The wound is an incomplete energetic cycle and, if left unresolved, it is perpetuated in other relationships and situations and can eventually manifest as physical illness and dis-ease within any body of consciousness...

Forgiveness is not about condoning an action that may have hurt you, but it is an understanding and honoring of why it occurred and the process of letting it go. It is not about forgetting what happened but about accepting what was and what no longer will be. Have you heard "I forgive you, but I'll not forget what you've done!" and it is said with malice and vengeance? Know that this is not True forgiveness.

Forgiveness is about moving from the past, which is dead energy, to the present of where you and the other are today. Did you learn, grow, and heal from your experience? ...

— Amanda Butler

Once you understand that there is no greater teacher than your struggle, you become appreciative of life. If my mother did not put me out, I would not be a survivor. I would not know how to depend on myself. If I never went to jail, I would not have the routine, structure, and discipline that is very much needed in life (these are the same skills you can pick up in the army or Navy by the way). It is about looking at the glass half full.

Once you understand that most people operate from their own fears, insecurities, and guilt, you no longer take things personally. When you know that you will never know everything and that life is an endless journey of learning, it humbles you. It took me some time, but again, I have realized that in every tough situation a whole lot of good came from it.

We only change and grow when we do not have a choice but to. I recommend putting yourself in situations where you have no choice but to adapt, grow, and evolve. Application, to sum it up. What you should have learned is that to begin to love yourself you must learn and understand where you learned love. Once you learn and understand the root behind why you are the way you are, you must move with an unyielding and unbreakable belief that you have the power to change your reality. I was able to remove the fear of my talents not evolving into success and becoming another waste of talent by removing the power I gave to people's opinions, mainly my mother's.

By making what I believe about myself a fact, and feeling it, not just thinking it, I understand that I am taking the actions to become who I want to be. So wherever I fall will be exactly where I NEED to be. I may not have said it, it may have been subconscious, but I believed people who told me that I am not who I am, especially when I looked at my situation, which reflected such.

And when you do not like who you are, you do everything you can to create an escape fantasy. This made it easy for me to disown my own flesh and blood and to accept someone in my life who would allow me to do so. But these are my kids, they did not ask to be here. Why am I punishing them for something they had no decision in making? Why am I beating myself up and feeling guilty for reflecting how poorly I was raised in my own actions? With that understanding, detachment, forgiveness, and the application of these laws, I stopped blaming life for being… well, life. And I am a better man because of it.

By now you should have written down what you are afraid of, insecure about, and feel guilty for. On the next page, answer the following questions.

What do you need to believe about yourself, and if executed, what could you accomplish?

_____

_____

_____

What is holding you back from believing in yourself?

_____

_____

_____

What do you need to detach from?

_____

_____

LOVE YOURSELF

Who do you need to forgive? Why?

"Most men make the error of thinking that one day it will be done.

They think, 'If I can work enough, then one day I could rest.' Or,

'One day my woman will understand something and then she will stop complaining.' Or, 'I'm only doing this now so that one day I can do what I really want with my life.' The masculine error is to think that eventually things will be different in some fundamental way. They won't. It never ends. As long as life continues, the creative challenge is to tussle, play, and make love with the present moment while giving your unique gift.

— David Deida

Part 2

The Trunk: Loving Yourself

SELF-LOVE IS BEING HONEST WITH YOURSELF, IDENTIFYING WHERE YOU ARE FUCKING UP AT AND RECTIFYING IT.

The beginning, the evolution

It was the summer of 1990. The artist's name was D-Nice. My father owned a 1988 Astro van and in the summertime, we would ride with the sliding door open. The aromatics of barbecue filled the air. There was a line down the block for the Apollo, vendors with African products filled the curb of the sidewalk, and thumping through the speakers as we drove up 125the street in Harlem was, "my name is D-Nice."

That was the day I fell in love with hip-hop. I was nine years old. Every time I heard that song I would run to the radio and try to record it, but I would always miss it. Until that one time… I was ready, I told myself I was not going to leave the side of my father's boom box until I recorded that song. I took one of my mother's old cassette tapes and waited with my finger on the "record" and "play" buttons. Luckily, the DJ was still running his mouth as the song was being introduced. I timed it exactly right and got a clean version. After recording the song, the next task was to write it down. I would do this for Slick Rick's *Children Story* and other artists until about 1994 when Method Man dropped his debut album. But that D-Nice song was the first song I had ever written down. To this day I can still hear the beat and the words…

LOVE YOURSELF

My name is D-Nice although I hate to admit it / Taking out you suckers and you don't know how I did it / See every episode, remains in this mode / Very cool, very calm, there's no sweat in my palm / I just, pick up the mic, proceed with a song / I get right to the point my competition's not long or short / It's like a sport, hanging in the middle / But now if you're puzzled, let me kick the whole riddle / That, my name is Derek, and if I didn't mention / D-Nice, is just a description / It describes, the kid on the mic / I'm the TR-808, huh, but just call me D-Nice.

— Derrick T. Jones

This is my earliest memory of writing something down that was not school related. I had no idea then, but it was in those moments the voice within began to speak to me. Where I began to gravitate towards what excited my being. An excitement that would take me on a journey and become the root of all I am as a writer…as a creative expressionist.

It was not until three years later that I would begin writing about my personal feelings, about unanswered questions regarding my biological father. After I was told by my parents and taken by my aunt to see him, that was it. I was left to try to figure out the rest of the story on my own. Paper became the listener; the pen was the voice and I observed from a short distance as the architect.

I began writing these feelings when I could articulate the pain. I guess all the years of writing down rap stories facilitated this process. As the years went by it seemed like the more pain I experienced, the better of a writer I became. The reason I say this is because what drove me to write my very first song was heartbreak.

I was incarcerated in Corrigan Correctional Facility in Connecticut in 1997. At the time, I was in a relationship with my first love. I called home to speak to my sister, but my mother picked up. I remember because of how not super excited she was to hear from me. I sat there in silence waiting for my sister to come to the phone. About a minute went by…

"Jamai," says Terry.

"What's up T? What's new?"

"I kind of have some sad news for you. I'm sorry."

"I'm listening. What happened?"

"I was walking in the school park over the weekend and I saw your girl kissing somebody by the swings. Come to find out your boy hooked it up too."

"Are you kidding me?"

"Yeah bro. I am sorry… Maybe I should have not told you because I know you are not here and cannot do anything about it."

"Do not think anything about it. You did the right thing. I'm your brother, you are not supposed to waste any time."

"Thanks. Let me go. I have to do something." I hung up the phone. I asked the officer if I could lock in early. I did not have anything to do, I just did not want to show how hurt I was over the phone, knowing it would make my sister feel like she should have not told me. I went straight for my bunk.

Carrying all that weight put me on my back, I laid there for hours. The pain from that hurt transformed itself into a song that wrote itself while I was asleep. That is the only explanation I can produce on why when I awoke, I was able to pour out these lyrics to an R&B song titled, "I'm the One." What is odd about this was I was never shown by anyone how to write a song. I did not know anybody doing music. I was only sixteen. And I have not stopped writing since.

Are there things that as a child you were good at that seemed to come from nowhere? You just had a knack for it. What was it?

_____

_____

_____

_____

_____

Are you in any way making a living from this gift? Is this natural ability a part of your life and passion as an adult? If not, why not?

_____

_____

_____

_____

_____

Many people mistake and confuse passion for a talent. Passion is not talent. Passion is the energy and desire to pursue. Here is how you can find or recognize what it is you are passionate about:

It is something you are willing to go to the end of the world to accomplish by any means necessary.

It is something you can do for hours without feeling lonely or tired. It is like an addiction. Something you always talk about. It consumes your life.

1. It can be making a difference in someone's life, being an educator, a teacher, or being a genuine person trying to help your neighbor. Whatever it is, it gives you a satisfaction unlike anything in the world.
2. Perseverance. Persistence. Patience. Positivity. It is something that no matter how hard it gets you keep pushing and never give up, to the point that one would question your sanity.
3. It is something that hurts so bad because you cannot seem to accomplish it, so you begin to wish that you never had the passion nor talent to pursue it in the first place.

What has sustained me all these years is my passion to pursue greatness, which fuels my ambition. It is what drives it all. Without it, it would be easy for me to give up, fall victim to pressure and circumstances. You must want it badly and prove it through your actions. It begins with thinking big. Thinking big requires strategy and time. It requires you to go through your progressions.

Life is not meant to be hard. It becomes hard when we do not embrace our uniqueness. Go back to your childhood. Think about the activities you did that put the biggest smile on your face. Focus on the things you could not stop thinking about. Hiding within your childhood fantasies, games, and activities, is the fabric of your fate. Know that the goal is to become free again. To unlock the chains of this system and enjoy your life. To have freedom. For your peace. I am an expressionist. Too creative to fit in a box.

I take words and give them life. I use language to create stories, which started with writing lyrics on a sheet. Music, poetry, books, and scripts are all expressions of my sufferings, joys, and pleasures; my world. Life has given me the greatest apprenticeship.

My passion has come from me dedicating my entire life to the visual and acoustic creation of many masters. I am every song to which I have ever listened. I am every movie I have watched. I am every book I have read. I am the cracks in the voices of an artist. I am the picture of their words. I am now drowning in my own orgasm because of it. I did not see it then, but everything we go through prepares us. It teaches us about people, ourselves, and how to deal with it all.

These lessons may seem like they have no point in your overall mission, but they do. That shitty job, your unsupportive friends, incarceration, homelessness, not having money, a clueless passion, all have meaning. Every experience you go through while in pursuit of your dream is molding you and is the untold story of your success.

If you are not pursuing anything but the same 9-5 routine, then you will feel lost. There will be a void. Especially the more stories you see of people following their hearts. It hurts knowing that you have not found what makes you special, but know that you are special. You are just too scared to step into the light in fear of hurting someone. You make excuses about why your happiness is not important. You let money and keeping up with the Joneses rule your decisions. You need to understand that without pain there is no gain. If the muscle does not tear, how can it repair itself and grow? You must break this cycle. Do not worry about starting over or starting from the bottom. Worry about dying with the feeling of not being able to see what you look like at your best potential.

> "Sooner or later something calls us onto a path. You may remember this 'something' as a signal calling in childhood when an urge out of nowhere, a fascination, a peculiar turn of events struck like an annunciation: This is what I must do, this is what I must have. This is who I am ... If not this vivid and sure, the call may have been more like gentle pushings in the stream in which you drifted unknowingly to a spot on the bank. Looking back, you sense that fate had a hand in it ... a calling may be postponed, avoided, intermittently missed. It may also possess you completely."

> "Whatever; eventually it wills out. It makes its claim... Extraordinary people display calling most evidently. That is why they are fascinating. Too, they are extraordinary because their calling comes through so clearly and they are so loyal to it ... Extraordinary people bear the better witness because they show what ordinary mortals simply cannot. We seem to have less motivation and more distraction. Yet our destiny is driven by the same universal engine. Extraordinary people are not a different category; the workings of this engine in them are simply more transparent..."

> — James Hillman

It all begins with you

My cousin Kionna invited me to a celebratory dinner party for her mother in the Bronx. I believe her mother had just received her Bachelor's degree. A huge accomplishment for a mother after raising seven children to adulthood. Although I wanted to help celebrate her mom, I had made up my mind that I was in for the night. I was not in a social mood. At least not until she suggested that I bring some of my books to sell. Then, my mood quickly changed.

By the night's end I had sold eight books at $15 each and made $120. Just coming off the dance floor, my cousin came up to me and pointed, "You see that gentleman sitting over there in the suit?"

"Yeah. That table of four?"

"Right. Take him a copy of your book. He works with kids."

My eyes lit up. I walked over and introduced myself.

"Good evening, Sir..." sitting out from the table towards the dance floor, he looks at me and smiles as I say, "My name is Jamai Wray, I'm Kionna's cousin. She told me to come over to see you because you may be interested in my work."

"Okay, what do you have?" he asks.

"I wrote and self-published my first book a few months ago. It is called *The Random Thoughts of a Philosophy Major Drop-Out: The Philosophy of My Life*. It is a book of short-stories, poems, parables, essays, comedy sketches, and journal entries chronicling my writing process and personal revelations and epiphanies. This spans over 13 years of my life experiences as a young man making every possible mistake you can imagine. Each piece has the month, day, and year with the age of its conception. It is not in chronological order, but it reads as one big story. I wrote it out of fear, which makes my tone very vulnerable and honest in the sharing of my emotions."

"Very interesting, you just sold that brother," he said. "Well my name is Kevin Allen and I work with the Department of Education, maybe I can help you out."

He took the book from my hand and began to skim through the pages. He looks up at me and says, "If I like it, I will change your life forever."

"Now that sounds great. Thank you. Can't wait." I signed the book, shook his hand, and joyfully headed back to thank my cousin.

"Hey cuzzo."

"Hey, how did it go?" asks Kionna.

"It went well. He said that if he likes it, he will change my life forever."

"He has been in DOE for a while now. I am positive he can make some moves for you."

"Well thanks for getting me out of bed and for the whole night. I'm happy I came out."

"Anytime cuzzo."

This was the week before the Super bowl. The year Joe Flacco and The Ravens beat Kaepernick's San Fran 49ers in a 34-31 stunner. So I had not expected to hear from Mr. Allen right away, but after a month passed, I began to lose hope. Immediately I thought about how vulgar and sexually provocative some parts of the book were. Then I started thinking about how working with him would work and what he could really do for me.

LOVE YOURSELF

I began to see how much the book was not for kids at all and discarded any remaining attention I gave to expecting to hear from Mr. Allen.

But then, in late March I received a surprisingly long-awaited phone call.

"Is this Mr. Wray speaking?"

"Yes. Mr. Wray speaking."

"Yes, Kevin Allen, I read your book. I love it man. 'Imagine that' is my favorite joint. You should tell your story. You are a champion at life."

"Thank you, Sir, that means a lot."

"Now of course you would have to clean it up some. But yes, I am going to set up a meeting with the principal at the school I work at so you two can meet. His name is Jamaal Bowman.

"Sounds great."

"Okay cool, catch up with you later," says Mr. Allen. Twenty minutes later I received a text from him that read, "check your email." Now you know I was super hyped then!

I checked my email and it was a W9 form to make me a vendor for the Department of Education. Shortly after, my phone started to ring.

"Hello?"

"Yeah, Mr. Bowman says there is no need to meet, he trusts my word on you. Congratulations, you're on your way brother," says Mr. Allen.

"Thank you, Sir, I really, really appreciate this."

"Yeah man, just stay in contact and let's do this."

"Will do."

By the first week of April 2014 I was in the system as a non-contracted vendor with New York's Department of Education. I was renting a room in Canarsie at the time. This was right before me and my old lady got an apartment together and guess what.

After all that, I let one entire year go by without reaching out to him. One entire year. I took no action. Not until that first full day alone in my apartment.

I was sitting at my desk with nothing to do, scrolling through my contacts when I finally acted. My ex had just left me the day before. I realized then I had spent most of my energy creating happiness for my lady and not for myself. As an aging man with lofty goals, what I need, as most men do, is status. To feel like a man. For me, that is being self-made. A creator and entrepreneur.

Being a man for me also entails doing what I want to do when I want to do it. To have control over my life and to depend solely on *my* efforts. A relationship is like a 9-5, women need attention and so does the relationship. With all that I needed to do for what I wanted to achieve, the relationship was a distraction.

The relationship required a lot of my time. And if you and your significant other do not have the same goals and share the same passions, then it is going to be exceedingly difficult for you to do you *and* sustain a healthy relationship. Not saying it is impossible, but it is extremely difficult. Looking back on how I was moving, I had shown myself no love at all.

I remember watching *The Great Gatsby* with my girlfriend and Leonardo DiCaprio's character said—and I'm paraphrasing this—"if he would have stayed with her it would have held him back. He loved her too much not to make her a priority." That scene will forever stand out to me because I did not know how to not make her and our relationship a priority. Plus, we had other issues that caused a lot of stress.

So the moment I was free from relationship duties, this huge weight lifted from my shoulders. There was nothing else to do but focus all my energy into building my brand and loving myself. Most importantly, *learning* to love myself. There is no way you can properly love another without properly loving yourself.

Making that phone call one year later to Mr. Allen in March of 2015 was the beginning of a lot of great decisions. He invited me to a Career Day one of the schools he works with was having. I had never spoken in front of kids before so preparing for that was a new challenge for me. The Career Day was not going to be until that May and before I could attend this career day, I had to meet with Principal Bowman first. The man who made me a vendor.

We all met at a T.G.I. Friday. Once introduced and settled in, Principal Bowman asks me, "If I allow you to come talk to my kids, what are you going to tell them?"

"I have this job interview piece I do where I show the importance of presentation."

"Nah nah, that is not it. If I let you speak to my kids, what are you going to tell them?" I sat there and really thought about this answer. And about how important answering correctly was.

I told him a story I never told anyone before. "It was my brother, my sister, my father, my mother, and myself at the dinner table. This was 1991, I was 11 years old. I asked my mother why I looked different from my siblings, my being darker and them lighter. She looked at me shockingly, as my question was clearly unexpected. My father did not budge.

The next day, a few hours after school, they told me to put my coat on and we walked down towards my school. I was nervous because the only time I went down to my school at that time of the day was if I was in trouble. I used to climb through the vents in my 5th grade classroom and was known for my theatrics, so I was afraid I had been found out.

Instead of going to my school, we stopped at the park and I sat on the bench. Looking up at my mother, she tells me that the man I had been calling daddy for the past 11 years was not my biological father. That he did not make me. That's why I look different from my siblings."

Before I could continue, Mr. Bowman said with enthusiasm, "Now that's what you go in there and you tell my kids because 95% of them can relate to that story. That is what you tell them after introducing your book. Be honest and transparent with them. Let them see themselves in you." After so many years of struggling just being me, I was now sitting across from a powerful man as my purpose was slowly being revealed to me. It was an awesome feeling.

May 2015 arrived and it was time for me to attend the Career Day. I was nervous, but prepared. I spoke to two 7th and two 8th grade classes. I told them the very story I told the principal and the amount of hands that went up for questions was astounding. Teachers were leaving the class calling other teachers. It was very apparent how magnetic authenticity really was. I remember telling the kids that I did not draft this book for them. That I wrote it for me. For my own sanity. To prove to myself that I can start and finish something.

I had learned that you do not find your purpose, you create it. I told them how by this point in my life I thought I would be the greatest rapper in the world. To be a rapper was the original plan and that I stand before them now because I never stopped writing. It grew into this because I continued to feed myself information on writing and I never stopped writing.

Out of all the presenters, I received the best evaluation and the school put in an order to purchase 100 copies of my first book. Though still heartbroken from my break-up, this gave me the distraction I needed. The wonderful thing about that whole experience was that I did not see any of it coming. It was a student's comment in one of the evaluations that really confirmed for me that I am, and was always on the right track, and that I can make an impact. That evaluation form and others are on the next page.

It blew my mind when I read this. His answer to question eight showed me that he got more than just my story. I planted a seed. I may have changed the course of his life forever.

Name of Presenter: April Wray   Date: May 15, 2015
Title of Workshop: Jamai

Overall, how would you rate this workshop?

1. How would you rate the usefulness of the content?
   (1   2   3   4   (5))
2. How would you rate the hands-on activities?
   (1   2   (3)   4   5)
3. How would you rate the presenter's knowledge in the subject?
   (1   2   3   4   (5))
4. How would your rate the presenter's style of teaching?
   (1   2   3   4   (5))
5. How would you rate the pace of the presentation?
   (Too fast   Too slow   (Just right))
6. Was the workshop above or below your current skill level?
   (Above   Below   (Just right))
7. What did you like best or find most useful about the presentation?
   I found the # books interesting and the book trailer
8. What skills did you learn that may help prepare you for technology integration in the classroom?
   I learned that you can make money by being yourself.
9. Were your personal learning goals for the course met?
   If "No," please describe those expectations that were not met.

10. Any other comments?

WORKSHOP EVALUATION FORM

Name of Presenter: Jania Wray   Date: 5/15/15

Title of Workshop: _____

Overall, how would you rate this workshop?

1. How would you rate the usefulness of the content?
   (1   2   3   4   (5))

2. How would you rate the hands-on activities?
   (1   2   3   4   (5))

3. How would you rate the presenter's knowledge in the subject?
   (1   2   3   4   (5))

4. How would your rate the presenter's style of teaching?
   (1   2   3   4   (5))

5. How would you rate the pace of the presentation?
   (Too fast   Too slow   (Just right))

6. Was the workshop above or below your current skill level?
   (Above   Below   (Just right))

7. What did you like best or find most useful about the presentation?

   He made everything relatable

8. What skills did you learn that may help prepare you for technology integration in the classroom?

   None (but he was an awesome person and writer)

9. Were your personal learning goals for the course met?
   If "No," please describe those expectations that were not met.

   Yes

10. Any other comments?

   You don't find a purpose you create it

WORKSHOP EVALUATION FORM

Name of Presenter: Jamai Wray   Date: 5-15-15
Title of Workshop: _____

Overall, how would you rate this workshop?

1. How would you rate the usefulness of the content?
   (1   2   3   (4)   5)
2. How would you rate the hands-on activities?
   (1   2   3   (4)   5)
3. How would you rate the presenter's knowledge in the subject?
   (1   2   3   (4)   5)
4. How would your rate the presenter's style of teaching?
   (1   2   3   4   (5))
5. How would you rate the pace of the presentation?
   (Too fast   Too slow   (Just right))
6. Was the workshop above or below your current skill level?
   (Above   Below   (Just right))
7. What did you like best or find most useful about the presentation?
   He was filled with information and knowledge.
8. What skills did you learn that may help prepare you for technology integration in the classroom?
   That you can't be successful by yourself.
9. Were your personal learning goals for the course met?
   If "No," please describe those expectations that were not met.
   Yes because I thought he was going to be boring but he was very interesting.
10. Any other comments?
    No

Name of Presenter: Jamai Hray Date: 5/15/15

Title of Workshop: _____

Overall, how would you rate this workshop?

1. How would you rate the usefulness of the content?
   (1   2   3   4   (5))
2. How would you rate the hands-on activities?
   (1   2   3   4   (5))
3. How would you rate the presenter's knowledge in the subject?
   (1   2   3   4   (5))
4. How would your rate the presenter's style of teaching?
   (1   2   3   4   (5))
5. How would you rate the pace of the presentation?
   (Too fast   Too slow   (Just right))
6. Was the workshop above or below your current skill level?
   (Above   Below   (Just right))
7. What did you like best or find most useful about the presentation?

   I like how Jamai compared his life to ours.

8. What skills did you learn that may help prepare you for technology integration in the classroom?

9. Were your personal learning goals for the course met?
   If "No," please describe those expectations that were not met.

   Yes

10. Any other comments?

    Jamai Hray is an inspiring man and I want to read more of his books.

LOVE YOURSELF

"Now that's what you go in there and tell my kids because 95% of them can relate to that story." Hearing Mr. Bowman's voice in my head after reading how this student loved how I compared my life to theirs meant that not only was he right, but that I was on to something. Up until this point, authoring the very book you see in this photo was the smartest move I had made.

In June 2015, I went to drop off 100 copies to the school. I took pictures with the students. I was so excited that I was sweating. Here is the actual photo from that day.

Right after I took this picture, Mr. Kevin Allen walked into the classroom.

"I have to show you something. This is going to blow your mind," he says. I was smiling from ear to ear because I had no clue what he was about to show me.

"I want to show you the impact you're already making. This is great."

What he showed me would change my life forever.

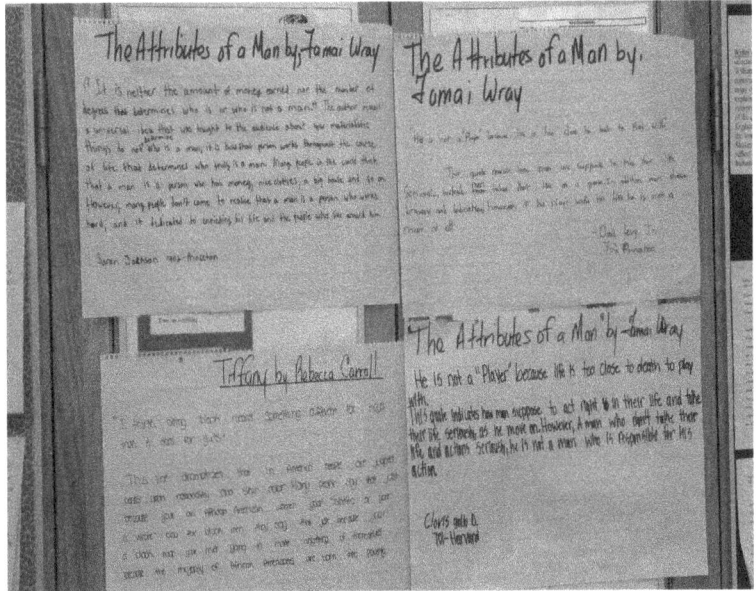

When I saw my name on that board my mouth dropped and I instantly teared up. I gave an English teacher a copy of my book a month prior and she took a piece I wrote and made a classroom assignment out of it. Mr. Allen introduced me to the class as the author and the kids went crazy. That was the lightbulb moment, and by the look on Mr. Allen's face, I knew he was thinking the same thing.

The students were asked to take a sentence from "The Attributes of a Man" and write what it meant to them, which was excellent because it made them think. After reading some of the paragraphs from the students I was amazed by how smart they were. Mr. Allen and I stepped out shortly afterwards. When we got in the hallway we looked at each other, paused for a moment, and he said, "You need to make a workbook. And not any old workbook either."

From that moment on I became his mentee. He told me about the workbook standards principals would be looking for based on Department of Education guidelines. He pretty much made sure all my T's were crossed and I's were dotted. He suggested that I research workbooks that had been successful. I purchased several workbooks from *Seven Habits* to *Chicken Soup for the Soul*, but I did not like what I saw in any of those books. They were not providing the structure I felt was needed to facilitate the rawness my life story contained. I wanted more of an open-ended discussion base format.

It was on June 26, 2015 when I began writing *The Random Thoughts Lifebook: A Personal and Social Awareness Life & Entrepreneurial Skills Program for Grades 8 Through 12*. I decided to structure my own template of how I learned things growing up. Things that made my vocabulary strong for example. I created a mantra - "if what you are reading does not require a dictionary, then you are not reading anything at all." Reading books where I needed a pocket dictionary handy is what grew my vocabulary. So why not start each lesson with a vocabulary building exercise, preparing students for the words they will be using during the day, with a glossary in the back? This was the very first idea and I was excited about it.

Seven months later in January of 2016 I completed my first draft. I had two workshops in a Bronx middle school called "Knowledge of Self." Here is where I would test my curriculum out for the first time. I started with the very first lesson in the Lifebook, "Presentation; you will be judged." For this activity I wanted to show the students that people will judge them based on the clothes they wear, by having the students judge me. But this workshop was not a classroom full of 8th graders. This workshop was principals, teachers, substitutes, and paraprofessionals. There I was, sitting at the desk with a robe and slippers on eating a blueberry muffin. One of the principals approached me as I was going to throw my muffin away and said, "Excuse me, check this, you are either a genius or you done lost all of your damn mind. I really can't wait to see which one it is." Boy oh boy, talk about pressure. I gave the whole lesson in my robe. Creating the judgment I wanted.

When I began my job interview activity my point began to reveal itself. In that activity the students were the employers and I was looking for a job, but I was not dressed properly. When I took the robe off and put my shoes on. Everything changed. Their judgment of me was different because I looked like the man for the job. The robe represented a distraction from my excellent resume.

Distraction can be anything from a sexual or drug related email, a tattoo on your face and hands, sagging pants, bad hygiene, etc. The life lesson here is simple, dress the way you want to be addressed. The class loved the lesson, but after two workshops I realized I had a lot more work to do. I had so much work to do that I did not finish the final draft of my workbook until a year later.

19 months later in January 2017, I completed a 273-page workbook with a teacher's manual. That same month I made my first sale to a middle school in the same district and my life has been changed since. Four years after meeting Mr. Kevin Allen in 2013 at my cousin's party, his words rang true. The separation between my ex and I was needed. Up until this point, being single was the best decision my ex could have done for me.

Because of my age and failures, I felt like I was behind in life, which made my craving for status that much stronger. If I was still in a relationship, I would not have written the workbook and manual while giving my lady and our relationship the attention it needed. Especially since our perspectives about success were different. She is the work-retire-and-pension thinker. I am an entrepreneur, my own boss, a retire-when-I-want thinker. But I am the one who needed to see this and make this decision myself. Because if she did not break up with me, would I have had the courage to step away from something that was not working? No. I honestly do not think I had the courage. I was willing to compromise who I was and what I wanted to accomplish in life for the sake of our relationship. Something she would have never done. I will explain a little bit more of that in a later chapter.

I consider myself blessed. Whatever my overall accomplishments will be must be stronger than the evils that could have kept me bound. Loving yourself is especially important. Focus is essential if you want to really exploit your gifts. It all begins with you. There will be no progression professionally or personally if you do not understand you are the beginning and the end. You are the creator and destroyer. You are the expert carver. You are nature simply disconnected from the ground, externally searching in places, things, and people rather than internally… connecting to the Earth that lies within you.

God can water and shine on your land, but only you can plant the seeds. It is more than a choice, it is a decision that requires a lifestyle change. Every ache and pain is a direct result of the separation of responsibility and accountability to yourself. My problem was that I expected my ex girlfriend to pay the tab for my happiness when it has always been my bill to pay. This gave her complete control over me. I was being controlled by my own expectations of making her happy, by giving her what I thought she wanted. But her happiness was not my tab to pay either. Her happiness should not be my happiness and vice versa. Happy couples are two individuals who bring their individual happiness to a relationship. The combination of the lack of love for myself, the lack of love I received from my childhood, and being conditioned to look outside of me for the answers is why I expected her to pay this tab. The same reason we expect our bosses and kids to do the same.

Unknowingly, we give other people the responsibility to make us happy. Because of the love your kids show you, a love you have not received as a child, you attach your happiness to theirs. Yes, your children's success should make you happy, but do not mistake the happiness from their success for the happiness you need to obtain for yourself. That is their happiness. This leads me to a question.

If you did not have any kids, what would you be doing to make yourself happy? I know a lot of young adults who say they live for their kids and that the source of their happiness is loving and seeing their kids happy. So what would you be doing for your happiness if you did not have any kids?

I made one phone call to Mr. Allen after my break-up and that one call released me from the prison I had locked myself in. It aligned me with people and events I needed to continue to show me the way. It was not until speaking to those students that I found my purpose. I am a teacher, an empowering force of inspiration. I had found the recipe of success.

What is the recipe of success? It is when you tie your talent and skills together and deliver it in the service of others with the intent to better humanity. Talent is your natural ability or gift in something. Like the ability to sing, act, or inspire. A skill is a learned ability acquired or developed after challenging work. To be in the service of others with the intent to better humanity speaks for itself and is our true purpose as humans.

My talent is the ability to write, inspire, and be creative. Learning how to author books, screenplays, and poems, and structurally use my creativity to produce a product is what makes me skilled. I took my talent and skills to the Department of Education to uplift the youth, to be the person I wish I had growing up. As I said before, it is our human obligation to take care of one another. This is how you give peace to the soul.

LOVE YOURSELF

We all have more than one talent. I believe everyone should make a living from doing what they are naturally good at. Not everyone is onboard with bettering humanity, but the formula of success is still the same. Here is how I used another talent of mine to make a living: I am extroverted, gregarious, and can make a stranger a friend within seconds of meeting them. Unbelievably, this is a talent. The only issue now is finding a field or an industry where I can monetize this talent. The first industry that came to mind was hospitality. The job, bartending. Bartending requires dealing with people. And since I am great with people, all I had to do was learn how to make drinks. Once I acquired the skill to make drinks, I was ready to go and make money. I created another source of income from what I'm great at and love to do. This is called monetizing your talent(s).

What is your talent(s)? (ex: writing, public speaking, networking, inspiring people, organization, etc.)

_____

_____

_____

_____

_____

What are you skilled at? Remember, skill is usually a developed talent. (ex: skilled writer, skilled critical thinker, skilled planner, etc.)

_____

_____

_____

_____

_____

What business can you create where you combine your talent and skill and use it to service others with the intent to better humanity?

_____

_____

_____

_____

_____

_____

LOVE YOURSELF

What industry/field can you get into where you can monetize your talents?

_____

_____

_____

_____

_____

_____

Mentorship

There is no better sign of humility and love for yourself than finding a mentor. Every time I thought I knew what I needed to know to move to the next level, I would run into a situation that reminded me I am not as informed as I think I am. This reminder began with how I viewed myself versus how people saw me. My theory has always been that it is not what I say but how it is received. Most of us do not have a clue about how we make people feel. I was so caught up in my own theories and arrogance I could not see how deprecating my actions were.

With a blind eye I was tactless for an exceptionally lengthy period, mostly from my late teens into my late twenties until I met my first mentor in 2007 at Gouverneur Correctional facility in upstate New York. I was 26 years old and standing against the wall in the dorm area of the unit when he came up beside me and said, "I knew one day I would meet you." Hearing this was the creepiest shit ever and being incarcerated with a bunch of men did not help. He went on to say,

"I heard you speak in the gym not too long ago and I knew the stars would align allowing us to meet. I don't know how much time we have, but before you leave here, I am going to let you know just how great you are." After he stroked my ego,

I was now intrigued and curious. He introduces himself, "My name is Herbert Sloan, nice to meet you. What's your name?"

"My name is Cheez."

"I didn't ask you what you call yourself. I asked you for your name."

"My name is Jamai."

"Good. You can call me Magic, Jamai. Now, I need you to teach me how to play chess."

"How do you know if I can play?"

"From how you speak."

In my mind I am saying the longest "okayyyy" because where did this man come from?

"It was in the gym a few weeks ago. You were having a conversation where one of the young men asked you a 'what if' question. The way you explained why you do not indulge in answering hypotheticals was genius to me. Especially since you are so young," says Mr. Magic.

"That doesn't support your assumption on my knowing how to play chess."

"But you do know how to play chess, so it is not an assumption. Grab that chair right there."

I grabbed one of the chairs at a nearby desk and we sat down. He unrolled the chess board onto the table and pulled the chess pieces out from a little pouch. "What does this piece do?" asks Mr. Magic.

"It's the Queen. It is the only piece on the board that can move in any direction with no limit. It stands next to the King to protect him. It is the strongest piece on the board, but second in significance to the King."

"Let us say the Queen is the woman. You heard the saying, behind every successful man there is a strong woman? She is your reflection. But instead of the Queen being a significant other, let her - for the sake of my point - serve as your mentor. The one who protects you from yourself, so you can reach your highest potential. You follow me?" asks Magic.

"Yes."

He points to the board again, "What is this piece and what does it do?"

"This is the Rook. It stands at the corners of the fortress and protects your weapons from being taken, as well as the outer perimeter from invasion. It can only move vertically and horizontally and works in concert with your firepower."

He looks at the piece as if it is talking to him. In deep thought he conjures another metaphor. "What do you do in your spare time, or to pass time rather?"

"I read and write."

"How often?"

"As much as I can until I get tired."

"Okay, so this piece called the Rook is your discipline and your structure and it protects the walls of your fortress, this fortress keeping your mind from being invaded by idle time. It is your focus that works together with your creativity. I see you are left-handed, what is your talent?" he asks.

"I write."

"Interesting. What is this piece?"

"It is the Knight. It is the only piece that can jump over other pieces but in an L shape. It is also the only piece that can make a move the Queen cannot. Like the pawn, it can initiate the first move."

"So let us say the Knight represents you avoiding your problems through erratic behavior. Risk-taking that sometimes works in your favor and at times does not. The complication of simplicity where instead of you breaking the wall down, instead of walking the journey and trusting the process, you choose shortcuts, to jump over it. You're with me?" says Magic.

"I follow you."

"Now, there's more of these pieces than any other, what is their purpose?"

"It's a pawn. It protects the front-line. With its limited mobility and power, it is almost sacrificial. It can only take another piece diagonally. Also, it is the only piece that when it reaches the other side of the board can bring back any piece to life. If I were to lose my Queen early, that would be a piece I would bring back. The pawns are often the last pieces to remain at the end of the game with the knight."

"So let us say this sacrificial pawn is the little guy. The one you talk down to and belittle. Telling them words doesn't exist like last night when you told one of the gentlemen you were playing monopoly with the word 'conversate' isn't a real word."

"Well, it isn't."

"I know that." says Mr. Magic. "But what was your purpose in telling him that word didn't exist?"

"Because I didn't want him to get caught out there looking stupid saying words that don't exist."

"So, your intent was good?"

"Yes. It always is."

"Do you think he knows your intent was good, based on how he responded?"

"I wasn't really paying attention."

"That is your problem. You do not see how you rub people the wrong way. Your lack of self-awareness and social intelligence causes you to complicate the simple exchanges you have with people by doing too much to impress and paint yourself more than you need to. In this case, assuming people want your advice or want to be corrected. Talking about yourself so much. You come off as if you are better than and if people receive you that way you will never reach your potential because you need people to be successful. Those who want to learn will seek you out. You must learn not to make people feel little. Calling people peons is not going to win you the crowd."

"You heard that?"

"Yes. Luckily, they did not know the meaning, or a fight would have broken out." We both laugh.

"I thought you didn't know how to play."

"I don't. I'm just here to let you know how great of a player in life you can be if you pay attention to how you move on the board—to your character flaws."

That was my first of many interactions with Magic. Magic spoke in parables and often walked with his arms wrapped around the back of his waist, which is why I do it now. He knew the Bible, the Quran, and all religions and history. But what was more intriguing was how much he knew about me. He had already served 16 of his 25 years in a federal prison and was doing the remaining of his time in the state. So he had already seen a lot. He captured my attention very quickly and we instantly became friends. It is incredibly hard to sum up all our conversations in retrospect, but one thing I do remember that stands out is what he told me the day after we met. We were walking to breakfast and he just came out and said, "Stop blaming yourself for why you're misunderstood in the eyes of your peers and seek to understand why that is the company you keep. If people do not understand you, then they were not meant to know you. You must surround yourself with like minds and not minds that lower your vibration. You are not wrong because you are wrong, but because you are outnumbered by ignorance. You need to read books on human behavior. Autobiographies of great successful people so you can see yourself in them. Continue to know you are great but know that you will never know everything. This is where your humility will be born."

One day we were at his cube and he asked me to get a dictionary. I grabbed the small one I had.

"What is your favorite word?" he asked me.

"Equanimity."

"Look it up in the dictionary you have."

"It's not here."

"Try this one." Magic handed me a much larger dictionary.

"Here it is."

"Now what is the definition?"

"It means mental or emotional stability, composure under tension or strain; calmness; equilibrium."

"Now if the word was in the first dictionary you looked for it in, what page would it have been on?"

I grabbed the first dictionary and skimmed through the pages. "It would have been on page 247."

"Take this bible and turn to page 247 and read the first sentence of each page and keep turning."

I turned to page 247 and began to read. As I began to catch what was happening, I was in awe. I could not believe it. Every sentence went together as if it was a paragraph defining the word equanimity. My mouth just dropped.

"How did you do that?"

"I didn't, you did. You have a strong purpose on this Earth. Whatever it is you will not see right now, but you are here for a reason. Like I told you earlier.

Before you leave here, I am going to show you how great you are. Let us go play some chess."

While we were at the table playing chess, Mr. Magic says, "I need you to write your life down."

"There's really not that much to write," I say.

"No, not what you have been through, but where you see yourself going. In detail too. From your impact, networth, homes you may own, kids, languages you want to learn, etc. Write it down. Make sure it is in tune with your passion and talent."

"And what is the lesson behind that sir?"

"It becomes reality when it leaves the mind and surfaces on paper. It will be your action and whether or not you give it your all will determine if it becomes a reality. But seeing it on paper makes you as a magnet that much stronger."

I honestly believe Mr. Magic knew how to play chess, but like the great teacher he was, he focused all his attention on me and never made it about him. He allowed me to be me without making me feel little or too exalted. Looking back on what Mr. Magic said and what I am doing now, I realize how significant a role model or mentor/life coach is to a young person finding their way. Someone to talk to them about life. We all need somebody to guide us, to save us from ourselves in a sense, but only you can do the work.

As much as I have studied and researched to write my workbook, it was the mentorship of Kevin Allen and Principal Bowman that put the icing on the cake. The added confidence and surety. The push. The advice for me to put the common core of ELA standards on the first page of the workbook is a clear example of guidance, of mentorship. Something I would have never thought to do. Nothing great achieved is achieved alone.

Get your shit together first

As a full-grown adult there are things you should know how to do and understand through practice and not theory before you ever think about being in a committed relationship. These six things are: how to cook for yourself, how to wash your clothes, how to be hygienic, how to manage your money, how to be loyal, and how to responsibly drink, if you decide to. These are things you should know how to do before romantically involving yourself with anyone.

Having your shit together also entails getting your education and career goals out the way: having a career in a managerial/supervision position, being an established entrepreneur, knowing how to lead yourself and make decisions, having direction, having an established and sustained way of living, and having structure and discipline. To be truly yourself, you cannot be weighed down by where your next dollar, job, or place of residence is coming from. Your focus and main priority should be on freeing yourself from these anxieties.

- Knowing how to cook for yourself makes you more resourceful to a potential partner. It adds to the important things that make up who you are. It raises your stock,

which becomes either your standard in a partner or not. Either way, this increases lifestyle. This is self-care/self-love.
- Hygiene speaks for itself. Next,
- 48% of Americans in both marriages and dating say they argue about money. As of 2018, 41% of Gen X marriages and 29% of Boomer marriages ended because of financial reasons. Finances are in the top five list of reasons why most relationships end. You must know how to manage your funds. Find stability so you will have security. This increases the success and longevity of a partnership.
- Lack of commitment, infidelity, and conflict/arguing are the number one cause for break-ups and divorces. So if you plan on playing around, don't. Practice what you preach.
- Every bad/negative encounter I had over the last 10 years all involved alcohol. From losing money, employment, and relationships. Know how to drink or do not drink at all.

If you are in your twenties, I recommend being alone for six years. This is for both men and women, I recommend not having any kids until around 30-40 years of age. It is important to grow beyond experiencing the physical pleasure of flesh and mature emotionally, financially, and spiritually enough to support yourself and a relationship. It is really about understanding who you are and the type of person you want to involve yourself with. Women, as you light, your shine makes a great man greater for it encourages him to think. Knowing who you are, doing what you love, and knowing where you are going really helps the stock of your genes. Your seed will get the best version of you when

LOVE YOURSELF

you allow yourself to ripen a bit. Learn what it is to be a man and ladies learn what it is to be a woman. Find a mentor, books, seminars, etc. Always seek mentorship for every aspect of your life until you are who you want and need to be for yourself and for your loved ones.

Love Yourself like you would love your significant other

Love is the greatest achievement. The union of man and woman is like the mating of the universe and all life. Look at man as the heavens and woman as the Earth. Look at man's seed as intelligence (thought) given to the ground (the womb) of the Earth. Through its giving, the womb receives and transforms this energy and information into the physical manifestation we call Life.

Your life force is the greatest example and expression of love in its purest form. The problem everyone has is that they want to meet the right expression of love and not take inventory of themselves, to see if they are expressing their most honest and purest self. It is impossible to receive the benefits the bond of love has to offer if you have not taken the necessary time to nourish and reach the level of comfort and contentment with who you are mentally and physically.

You cannot go looking for the right person until you yourself have become the right person. You must be able to meet your own requirements. Too many of us get into relationships before we learn how to love ourselves, before we have a healthy relationship with ourselves. We say we know what we want before we even know who we are.

LOVE YOURSELF

If you continue to avoid loving you, then why *wouldn't* the universe continue to send you someone who avoids loving you too? With this understanding, the first thing I did after I stopped beating myself up, after I stopped drinking my life away in sorrow, was go to the Barclay's Center for a Mother's Day Concert to see Keyshia Cole, Ginuwine, Monica, Avant, Joe, and Tank.

This is something I thought I would never do by myself. I thought going to the movies by yourself was a crime at one point in my life. But I realized, if you can shower your significant other with this type of date, then why can't you love yourself the same way? Everything I did for my ex I began to do it for myself. I went out to nice restaurants. I went to cool events. I began loving and treating myself in ways that I would for someone else I loved romantically.

Let me ask you a question: How do you feel about life right now? What are some of the things you do not like about yourself? Please, be honest.

THE FOLLOWING ARE RESPONSES FROM STUDENTS AT A MIDDLE SCHOOL I TEACH AT WHEN THEY WERE ASKED THE SAME QUESTION.

05/10/2018

I feel like I got the ability to be successful but certain things is getting in the way but even when I get a chance to change I dont take it as a priority.

"The way I feel about life is mixed because I feel like I would have all the tools or roads to what I want to chase in life, but my mom is holding me back from doing what's actually good for me. I say this because whenever there is a good opportunity for me, my mom would mess it up by either telling me to go home early or telling me to not to go at all.

5-20-18

Dear Ocean

The way I feel about life is mixed. It's mixed because I feel like I would have all the tools or, roads to what I want to chase in life, but my mom is holding me back from doing what's actually good for me. I say this because whenever there's a good opportunity for me, my mom would mess it up by either telling me to go home early or telling me to not go at all. On top of that, she wants me to go to a charter school all about education, no gym, and the gym is what lets out all my stress and it's what relaxes me. So I don't know how to feel in situations like these when she doesn't allow me to do me.

On top of that, she wants me to go to a charter school all about education, no gym, and the gym is what lets out all my stress and it's what relaxes me, so I don't know how to feel in situations like those when she doesn't allow me to do me."

I feel unique and I feel like nobody understands me or supports me in what I want to do. I feel like people take advantage of how nice I am.

"I feel unique and I feel like nobody understands me or supports me in what I want to do. I feel like people take advantage of how nice I am."

5/10/18

I feel like I'm on my way to the path of success because my grades are looking good and the school I'm attending is or has a good basketball program that I think I will fix in good but I have friends and cousins that I like hanging around. But those friends be getting in do trouble and like robbing, fighting, and smoking. They also want re to go to their high school. So, I don't know what school do go to.

"I feel like I'm on my way to the path of success because my grades are looking good and the school I'm attending is or has a good basketball program that I think I will fit in well with. But I have friends and cousins that I like to hang out around, but those friends be getting into trouble and like robbing, fighting, and smoking. They also want me to go to their high school. So, I don't know what school to go to."

5/10/18

I feel like im still a kid b I have to mature in order to get this scholarship & I have to increase my effort in school & I feel like im trying to become a man but I have no man to help me with my life because my pops left & my brother don't like me my moms picks my brother over me & my grandma is by my side I feel motivated to make it to the nba because somebody on my block motivates me

"I feel like I'm still a kid and I have to mature to get this scholarship and I have to increase my effort in school and I feel like I'm trying to become a man, but I have no man to help me with my life. Because my pops left, and my brother does not like me. My mom picks my brother over me and my grandma is by my side. I feel motivated to make it to the NBA because somebody on my block motivates me."

LOVE YOURSELF

After the class I took the same route home I take every day - walk up Webster Avenue to Grand Concourse to hop on the D train at 167th street, then take it to 7th and 53rd street and catch the E to Jamaica Center. On the E train is when I pulled out the letters and began to read them.

Letter 1 is all about self-awareness. The student is aware that he can achieve success. He knows there are things in his way and owns up to not making change a priority when the opportunity presents itself. Positives: Awareness, accountability, confidence. Diagnosis: lack of motivation.

The great part about this activity is the fact that he is not in denial, which means he is teachable. At this moment in his life, he needs an environment that encourages him to be the best version of himself. He needs to be reminded how great he is and how great he will be.

He already believes it, but this belief in oneself can lose its power if not given the proper information for cultivation. This is where the problem lies. Getting the right information to these kids involves creating routines and providing structure. They need to be taught how to motivate themselves because a lot of them cannot rely on it from anyone else. These kids are not bad. They just are not getting the proper information.

When I got to **Letter 2**, halfway through reading I began tearing up. "I feel like my mother is holding me back," he said. Wow. I had to pause and catch my breath after reading that line. Here it is, an eighth grader, going through exactly what I was going through, who feels like his mother is stopping his evolution.

When I was 23 years old, I had lost a job as a utility worker at a milk plant in Jamaica, Queens and I needed to move back home with my mother. Lucky for me, my mother and my sister needed assistance with watching my nephew. I would watch him when my mother went to work until his mother - my sister - came in from school. So me living there was a win-win. It was difficult to find work and I was making music at the time, so a friend and I pooled our money together and decided to get into the party promoting business.

We threw a party and even my mom showed up. It was a tremendous success. I tripled my money and could not wait to throw another one. Right after the party, the next morning when I came home (I had stayed out that night) my mother would not let me in. She told me she didn't want me living there anymore. I could not believe it.

What mother shows up to her son's party, dances, has a fun time, and then kicks them out the day after? I was not doing or selling any drugs in her house. I was not bringing any women to her house. I respected her wishes. Now some of you may say, there has to be more to this story. A mother is not just going to kick her son out for no reason. Party or no party. So I had to have done something, right?

Wrong. All I did was triple my money and was willing to give her half of it. Was willing to give half of what I was worth for room and board just to have peace. I was on to something so giving up half of it did not matter to me, but it was not about the money. It was about her not agreeing with how I wanted to live my life. It was about how I was spending my money. I wanted to go into party promotion and she did not agree with that. But to kick me out…

I slept at a friend's that night and when I came back to get my belongings, she would not give them to me. She just told me no and shut the door. Her refusal led to me calling the police. I had no other choice in the matter, I needed my stuff. When the police officers arrived, I explained the situation and they sided with me and told her to give me my belongings. As I went to get my bag, right in front of the police she smacked me in my face.

LOVE YOURSELF

They restrained her and asked me what was really going on here. I explained all the events that led up to this and I kid you not, one of the police officers asked me for my autograph.

My mother frowned and her exact words were, "he ain't nobody." The police officers asked if I wanted to press charges and I said no. "I did not come here to get my mother locked up, I came here to get my belongings." And for the next two weeks, I was homeless.

I tried my hardest not to look at my mother's actions negatively, but it seems so wrong to even think a mother could feel this way about her child. But when I reflected on her upbringing and understood the kind of person she was, I realized that it is not impossible nor is it unheard of. Just, why me? Why must things be so difficult for me?

It only served as poison to continue denying the truth staring right at me about my mother and the situation. My mother's actions did not make any sense nor did it define me as being wrong or dumb or anything negative. It took me years to realize that that was not a "ME" issue.

So going back to the student, it was difficult suggesting what to do and how to handle his situation with his mother because he lived under her roof. So instead, I suggested that we set up a meeting between his mother and I.

I was not going to assume that his mother was purposely preventing him from doing what he loves. I wanted to see how she viewed things. There was probably just a problem with communication and expression. The mother agreed and we met. I discovered there were more issues going on than what I gathered from her son's letter. What I learned was that, in her eyes, she was trying to stop him from becoming like his father. Any activity he tried to involve himself in where social influence and peer pressure was likely to be present, she felt she would lose him and did not want him to be involved in it. She thought she was helping him, but *he* felt she was hurting him. And the mother was delivering her opinions in a manner that contradicted her intent.

The child never knew this about his mother and the mother never understood this was how he viewed her. For the mother, she had to detach herself from the root of her and her son's issue, which meant dealing with how she feels about his father. Once she dealt with that, she had to learn to trust her son to be responsible. This made his rope longer. I recommended them to a doctor I work with for further help because I knew that their problem could be fixed.

There are four different issues in **Letter 3**. One, the student feels that he is unique. For me, that equals confidence. To see your separation from your peers and with the choice word "unique," he knows he is special. Two, he feels like no one understands him, which points to him looking for acceptance from others. He wants to be understood by his peers. I suffered from this all the way into my mid-twenties.

When it is clear that you are not like the rest, you want people to understand that you are not so different at all, but one of the dreadful things about looking for acceptance from others, especially when you are young, is that you tend to alter who you are to fit in. You do not know the beauty of uniqueness yet. He was seeking the approval from others to validate who he was and placing too high a value in the opinions of others.

This energy needed to be extracted to nullify the value of others' opinions and redistributed into cultivating his future, his growth. Third, he felt like he was too nice. Probably because he was taught to always be nice and kind. Initially, I wanted to tell him that he should not worry about that right now, focus on your grades and schooling. But that is exactly the problem, brushing it off does not get rid of the problem. We were all brought up to not speak about ourselves in a glorifying manner. We've been told that no one likes a person who is not humble or modest. The only problem with that is, in most cases, you end up not believing in yourself. When chasing your dream or building your brand, if you do not think you are the baddest motherfucker walking on Earth, no one else is going to believe it either.

Attraction requires action. There are a lot of healthy attributes and virtues in believing in oneself, in believing you are the baddest motherfucker walking the Earth. Do not let the words "cocky" or "selfish" or "arrogance" define nor disparage you. Always voice when you feel your kindness being taken for weakness. You must be you. It is the only way to vibrate high enough to attract the lifestyle you want when you act.

There is nothing wrong with walking with your chest out. Own who you know you are, even if it feels distant. See your future self in confidence and pride. Even if no one sees it but you. The Universe is still laying the foundation from your thoughts. Focusing your energy on people liking you wastes the energy you could be putting into yourself.

This can cause depression and disable any efforts you may have on becoming the person you want to become. There are kids who not only feel the way you do, but who are special and unique just like you. Something I was told as a 26-year-old by my mentor, Magic, is that if you continue to be who you are and not worry about why you are misunderstood, read avidly, continue to be confident and nice, but do not allow yourself to be taken advantage of, you will create a vibration of authenticity and bring those who are just like you around.

Never vibrate at an energy that does not reflect who you know you are. All the people who you want to define you, vibrate at a frequency not conducive to you. Popularity is an illusion of happiness. Looking for acceptance lowers what you think you are worth. Some people are just not going to understand you and that's okay.

Which leads me to the fourth issue: support. As simple as I can put this, and I said this earlier on, it is *your* dream. It is what you want to do. No one can see into your head. The number one support you will need and all that matters is the personal investment you make. Most people cannot support their own dreams or even themselves. They barely even know who they are and you want support from them?

If no one supports you, should you stop pursuing happiness? Are you supposed to quit and give up because your mother, brother, best friend, or sister will not put the same energy you put into your dream? Does that mean you should call it quits? No. Nothing worth it is easily attained. Life will constantly thrust you into situations where you question yourself, your friends, family, business partners, and others. Always be you. There is no one counting on this more than you. At least have respect for your future self if you do not have respect for yourself right now, because 10 years from now they are going to wish that you cared.

Letter 4: One of my favorite chapters in my workbook is "Friendships and Understanding Relationships." This student is aware that the very friends and family he likes hanging around are no good and that they will be going to the same high school he wants to attend, which will make it difficult for him to stay focused. The beauty of the situation is that he understands that strength is built in adversity. So if he wants to go to this school because of their basketball program, although the peer pressure will be high, this is where he can work on his discipline and self-control.

Your friends now will most likely not be your friends later. Whenever I begin this lesson, I begin it with that statement. If it were not for Facebook, I would not have any kind of relationship with some of my childhood friends. Families move, people change and grow apart and that is fine. In some situations, you will find yourself having to choose between what your gut is telling you is not healthy and the courage to love yourself more. Do not be scared. Always choose self.

Letter 5: No father, no male role model, no mentor, no guidance, and more than likely no resources except one person in his neighborhood that motivates him. Here is a young man who wants to be a man, yet knows he has no examples as a resource. He is aware of the mental and social poverty he is going through. He is aware of what he must face in his community and knows he must remain positive.

After reading his letter, I continued to diagnose his situation and find solutions to get him what he needed. I shared the same story - lack of proper leadership and turning to literature also saved my life. I found what I had been missing by reading. I learned who I was by reading. I saw myself - my behavior, my story, my emotions, sadness, and experiences - in what I was reading and that is what helped me change my life around. I applied what I now understand about myself to be my best self.

Just like the young leader from letter 1, he is teachable. He also needs an environment that encourages the benefits of being the best version of himself. He needs information and resources from strong positive Black men. He needs to see examples of his greatness in others.

So my advice to you is to find someone who has the qualities you seek, a person who is in the position you want to be in and ask them how they got there. And when I say position, I mean happy. There are many people who have been in the same exact situation you are in right now and made their happiness a priority. Seek them out because you need help to get to your destination.

Think about some of the things you complained about as a child regarding how you were raised. Can you name a few things you still deal with today that stem from long ago? Have you honestly taken care of it? Do you still blame someone or something else?

_____

_____

_____

_____

_____

What do you feel needs to be done to make things better?

_____

_____

_____

_____

_____

Self-awareness and the Ego

Self-awareness is understanding who you are, what your strengths and weaknesses are and how you got to be that way. It is understanding how your presence and/or behavior affects others. It is how you accurately perceive your emotions in the moment. It is finding the core behind your triggers. In mentorship, when I was telling the story about Mr. Magic pulling my card on correcting a fellow inmate's grammar while playing Monopoly, when asked why I did it, my answer was…

"I didn't want the brother saying words that didn't exist and embarrass himself…my intentions were good." Well, that was a lie. That was my ego's reason. The truth of the matter is, I wanted to be right. I was always told what I could not do as a youth. That my head was too far in the clouds. That I was a pipe-dreamer. That I was not who I thought I was. Because of this, every time I had a chance to be right, I took it.

It took me years to understand how much control my ego had over me. How truly traumatized I was. I held on thinking that I was purely doing things out of my good intentions for years, until I finally understood how far the ego would go to protect itself. Your ego is not you. Your ego tries to keep you from you. The ego never wants to feel embarrassment.

It was not until I was no longer embarrassed by my story or by anything for that matter, that I saw how much real estate my ego owns. This is what truly being self- aware is about. Saying that my intentions were good was my ego trying to look good in a bad light. It was my ego saying, "okay, he got mad, but it was not my fault, my intentions were good."

The ego never wants to admit when it is wrong. It always finds a way to take the blame from itself and put it on others and outside forces. If you cannot say sorry and come to terms with being wrong sometimes then you are in grave danger. You are human and flawed like us all. It's okay. My advice to you is that if you are having this problem, then place yourself in embarrassing moments. This is how you free yourself from your ego. The moment you can laugh at the same things that once rubbed you the wrong way, is the moment you are no longer controlled by your ego and people's opinions.

Another way to determine whether or not your ego runs your life, is to think about how you look at feedback and criticism. I always said, "it's not what I'm saying, it's how you're taking it" or "It's not my fault you took it the wrong way, that's a 'YOU' issue."

But, yes, it is my fault. How selfish and egotistical am I to not see that my satisfaction comes at the expense of someone's discomfort? How selfish am I not to care about another person's feelings? How egotistical am I to always defend a lie so that I am not embarrassed? I used to get angry and upset when someone gave me feedback or any kind of criticism with which I did not agree. I viewed them as haters. But the truth of the matter was that my ego was bruised.

LOVE YOURSELF

Do you have a problem with saying sorry to people when you're wrong?

_____

_____

_____

_____

_____

_____

Does it upset you when people correct you?

_____

_____

_____

_____

_____

_____

Does it bother you when you did not know something others thought you knew?

_____

_____

_____

_____

_____

_____

Are you a person that corrects people?

_____

_____

_____

_____

_____

_____

Confidence: You must want something

Just imagine the amount of confidence I had to be able to say to myself, "you know what, I am going to write a curriculum and get it distributed throughout the New York City Department of Education and Charter school system. I do not care if I lack credentials or have a criminal past. My past does not define me. I know authenticity to be king. This is who I am. This is what I know. There is no such thing as impossible. I am going to get this done and be a leader in urban education. I have a doctorate from life."

So where does all this confidence come from? The activator of all success comes from those who see it. Those who feel it and those who really want something from life. Wanting something is what creates the energy to pursue it. The confidence to get it and the belief that you deserve it comes from paying attention to how the world works.

What do I mean by that? Look at all the examples from Mark Zuckerberg to Bill Gates and the countless success stories of people who have had enormous success without a degree. Actors who never took classes and became huge stars. Knowing that these people were in my same position at one time is what gave me confidence. If they can do it, why can't I?

Doubt in yourself will only alter the people, circumstances, and events needed to deliver you what you desire. There is nothing new in this simulation of life. It was, is, and will always be the same. My confidence sits on the foundation of this understanding. The only thing that can get in my way is me.

If you want to become better at identifying these things, if you want to obtain these habits, then hang around people who have developed this understanding and perspective in life. Read autobiographies on entrepreneurs and innovators and you will see yourself in them. Confidence is knowing if you keep pushing, you are going to get to where you want to be because greatness comes from the seed of consistency.

What glitters is not always gold

With my confidence at an all-time high, it was time to get out there and get my curriculum in every school I could. It was time to hustle. Still delivering milk, I would begin my day at 2:30am, get on the train, make my deliveries, and be back home by 9:30/10am at the latest. I would shower and shave, get dressed, and take the E train from Jamaica Center to the D train at 7th Avenue, to the Bronx, three times a week. I did this for months.

One day at work while serving a stop on my route. I realized there was a charter school on the other corner of the same block. The famous Harlem Children's Zone on 125th Street and Madison Avenue. I told myself if I see anybody come out with a staff shirt on, I am going to approach them about getting my curriculum in their school.

I stepped down off the truck. Case by case I dropped the milk onto the hand truck. As I went to wheel it inside the store, I saw a woman about to cross the street with a Harlem Children's Zone staff shirt on. I stopped and walked towards the intersection, palm out for a handshake.

"Excuse me, my name is Jamai Wray. I'm a vendor for the Department of Education, can you lead me to the person who can help me get my curriculum inside your school?"

"You're looking at her. I am the High School Coordinator. You have 60 seconds. I'm just going to move my car."

"I created a curriculum that teaches life lessons to build character and morale based on my life experiences. I also created a teacher's manual to go along with it. Topics range from how to present yourself, how to effectively communicate, navigating friendships and understanding relationships, fear, the art of listening, emotional intelligence, self-awareness, teamwork, the power of humility, and the mental struggle that comes with following your dreams and ends with triumph. I'm currently in two middle schools in the Bronx, in negotiation with the Osborne organization to get me and my curriculum on Rikers Islands for the young men detained, and my mission is to be the person I wish I had growing up."

"Okay, very impressive. Bring your resume to the front desk and leave it for me. My name is . I'll be in contact."

"But my resume only reflects jobs I had driving trucks and buses."

"Then just put down everything you just said to me. That is your resume right there."

"Okay. I will. Thanks."

"No. Thank you."

I sprinted back to my truck and delivered the milk to the store with a huge smile on my face, thinking that all I needed was an interview. Just one interview. Four days later on a Tuesday, I received a phone call for an interview. Ah man was I hyped. I got to the interview and it was three of us. I was interviewed by the middle and high school coordinators.

Every question I answered to perfection. I had them fighting over me. I was so damn good. So good that they went up and got their boss to show them my workbook, which I called *lifebook* since it is about life. He was impressed after a few questions. Two days later, HR contacted me to let me know I was nominated for the position.

Working Mondays to Fridays 3:00pm -7:00 pm for them was not my initial intention. I didn't want to. I wanted to work *with* them, I am a business. I went through orientation and was sent to the Department of Health at 65 Court Street for fingerprinting. I was so excited because I believed that once I got into this particular school, I could get into all schools in New York City.

The last part of the process was to gain security clearance. So now I was just waiting for my appointment date. Once I was cleared, I could begin working.

I was home one afternoon going over the employee's handbook, reading about all the benefits and rewards and help with furthering your education was astounding to me. This is a real company. And then I read something that told me, if I were to implement my curriculum while at work, I would have to sign over my rights of ownership to Harlem Children Zone. Oh hell nah, nope, not happening, I cannot take this job. A check for a million dollars would not excite me or change my mind. This was my baby. My story. My legacy.

That following Monday I received a notice letting me know that I did not get cleared to move along the hiring process because I was still on probation, which they consider an on-going situation.

Being on probation saved my ass. Just imagine, if the universe did not save me from this glittering gold-plated mess I almost walked into, they would have had all legal rights to go after my curriculum once hired and implemented. I mean, they were hiring me because of my curriculum so I would have lost that case. My signature was already on the dotted line.

I'm simply happy it is over and I can relay to you that not everything that glitters is gold. There are certain gold chains you should not put around your neck because you will not be able to remove the infection that rash is going to leave on your neck. Do what you love, but never sell your soul, your booty hole, or sacrifice a family member's life to get there. Your transition to the next realm will not be pleasant.

Self-preservation

There is nothing wrong with putting yourself first. There is nothing wrong with looking out for you. In fact, understanding this puts you that much more in a position to be selfless. It is okay to help others, but when it interferes with your development and ruins the chances of experiencing the gratifying joy that personal and entrepreneurial accomplishments bring you, it is a problem.

The word selfish is always the term associated with putting yourself first, but this is not about having an abundance of something and being unwilling to share. It means putting you and whatever necessitates your path to success and happiness first. I was so much in love with my ex that I was willing to compromise the focus and attention required to pursue my dreams and be happy, just to be in love and ensure her happiness. All because I thought making her happy would make me happy.

It was Christmas 2014 when my ex and I got into an argument over my paying the cell phone bill of my kid's mother. She said she could not deal with me anymore and left because I always put my kids' moms first. Her reasoning at the time was suspect, but I could not prove otherwise. The truth of the matter was that I did not get anything for my kids that year, and my kids' mother saved my image by signing a few present labels from daddy.

When I explained this to my ex, she did not believe me and on February 1, 2015, I came home to an empty apartment. I received an email from her a few weeks later stating that she needed a favor. She wanted me to lie to the interviewer about her time with me because we shared an apartment. Since she was in the process of becoming a police officer, and I was a felon, she couldn't have any affiliation with me. And in this favor is where I found out the truth on why she really left.

But what is sad about this whole thing was that one year prior to our separation, we had a conversation about her becoming a police officer. I told her if she ever were to become a police officer, I would not want to be with her. The reason being, besides my not liking the gang culture of the police department, was why she wanted to be a police officer in the first place.

For her it was all about the money, benefits, and pension. But a job that requires you to wear a vest and gun every day is a job you do if you really want to combat crime. You must be willing to die for that badge. It should not be about the money. On top of that, I also told her that because of my past, we would not be able to be in a relationship. And it was in that car, in that very moment driving through the Battery Park tunnel, when, in her mind, unbeknownst to me, she ended the relationship.

A few months after that conversation we got an apartment together. An apartment where she never paid any rent. The only contribution she made was to the living room, TV, and bedroom set, which makes sense now because those were the things she took when she left. It was all planned.

I could not even be bitter because I respected it so much. I was even jealous. She put herself first. She exercised self-preservation at my expense and did not let her love for me stop her from achieving what she had to do for herself. I, on the other hand, was too understanding and too tolerable.

Sell the experience

The most important skill you must acquire as early as possible, preferably during your 20s, is your selling skills. A huge part of understanding yourself is having the ability to sell yourself. You are the product. Your story is your brand. The confidence you display when meeting with people either creates a high ceiling of possibilities or a low roof of missed opportunities.

When I first met Darren, my curriculum was not completed. All I had was my book. Being that the idea to write the workbook came shortly after I sold my first copies to a school, I wasted no time creating it. This stranger, later colleague and now friend, wanted me to let him know when I had finished the book because he would help me push it in schools. He became my inside guy. He kept me updated on what was going on. Helped me learn the lingo spoken throughout the Department of Education, which presented me as someone who had experience.

He was cool with a business manager. Through this business manager I would know what schools received money for programs that fit the criteria of my program and how much funding was allocated. Being that he had worked in the DOE for eighteen years, his knowledge on the schools that would love my program served me well.

In April 2017, he called me and said that there was a school looking for my services. He set up the conference call and I got the gig. This made my third account since releasing my workbook and an opportunity to launch my program.

October 2017, Darren sent me to a school where he knew someone close to the principal who could get me a meeting. The reason it is imperative to know someone on the inside is because principals are usually off limits. There were many times I went to a school and was there for only a few minutes, barely getting a chance to set up a meeting.

I met with his guy, gave him the speech I gave everyone along with a copy of the laminated table of contents I created as my business card with all my information, and waited. I did this because every school I went to would try to keep my workbook, and though protected through its copyrights, I could not have that.

One month passes by, nothing. I went back in November and met with a director of an outside program Mayor DE Blasio set up for renewal schools. The meeting went extremely well. She was impressed with my program, loved the videos of me facilitating the program, and said she wanted me to work with 60 students. I would just have to wait for the budget to come in because this was going to cost them $6,000.

After the Thanksgiving holiday I went back to the school for an update, nothing. She said she was still waiting for the budget, but she would be in contact. With the Christmas break approaching and the focus strictly on the holidays, I did not go back to this school until January 29. This time I met with the school's business manager.

I broke down my program and she said she would be in touch. A week went by and I emailed her, nothing. At this point Darren was furious because he could not understand why people would say they want to work with me, but never reach back out. He wanted me to try his first contact one more time. The guy I went to see in October. This time, he said he texted the principal a link to my videos and guess what, *still* nothing!

I told Darren I was going to three schools in that district that day. He suggested I try the school one last time. I said okay, but I was going to pop up with flowers and candy and see if it gets me in because it was Valentine's Day. I made sure I was clean as a whistle. I bought four roses and a box of chocolates from Walgreens. I went to the school's main office to see Principal Jane. One of the staff members took me to see the principal. She asked me politely to wait outside. I was nervous and my palms were sweating. It was unusually hot for some reason.

One minute later I was walking into the principal's office.

"Happy Valentine's Day. These are for you."

"Are you serious?" she asked.

"Yes. It is Valentine's Day. It would have been a travesty if I came empty handed. Now I did not want to get you one rose because I would have been playing myself. I did not want to get a bouquet because I did not want to make your significant other jealous. So, I thought four roses were simply fine." The smile on her face said it all.

"How may I help you?"

"My name is Jamai Wray. I am a vendor and have been for four years now. A memo came across my desk last month of schools who received funds for the young men initiative and peer-to-peer mentoring programs and your school is on the list. I would like to show you how my program fits the criteria."

She sat back as I went on to explain my program. The origin of it. How and why I began writing. My lung surgery. Incarceration. Homelessness. My mentors and what schools at which I had taught.

At the end of it, she was blown away.

"How do you know how to do all this," she asked. I just shrugged my shoulders. But the next thing is what made my heart race. She said she wanted to show me something. She turned her computer around and asked me to read the email she just sent to her staff. As I read, I could not help but to slowly see that just three hours prior to my being there, she was asking her staff to help her find a vendor for the very memo I showed her. She had not spent any of the $28,000 allocated. My mouth dropped.

"Wow. If that is not God, I do not know what is."

She said she would be in contact whether she planned to move forward with me or not. I was planning on hearing something the next day to be honest with you. That is how good the interview I created for myself went.

But one week went by and nothing happened. That Thursday, February 22, 2018, Darren called me saying that his boy hit him up saying that the principal had been emailing me, but it was getting sent back to her. I began to panic. This could not be happening. What if she went with someone else already? And because of my schedule and other responsibilities I could not pop up at the school until February 28.

I went that Wednesday with what I heard was her favorite tea from Dunkin Donuts, Vanilla Chai Latte. I walked into a huge smile as I placed her tea on her desk.

"You are good Mr. Wray."

"Thank you."

While in her office she showed me the email she had sent me and its return to her. I immediately knew what the problem was, the first letter in my first name could be mistaken for an "I." I gave her the address of my Gmail account and she forwarded it to me. Come to find out, she sent the email you are about to read the very next day after our meeting as I thought she would, this is what the email read…

LOVE YOURSELF

"Good morning Mr. Wray, My business manager will reach out to get the ball rolling. Brainstorming an effective partnership: We are planning to spend the $28,000 on your services, unless directed to do something else by the district office or 9X9. Here is what I am thinking: One on one mentoring sessions with identified 6th, 7th, and 8th grade overaged students."

Wait, oh…my…God. She is going to spend it all with me. I never jumped so high and screamed so loud with joy, without physically showing it, in my life. I had to force myself to be calm and professional and act like I was used to this kind of business and money even though I was not. The only hurdle was because I am a non-contracted vendor, I could not receive more than $25,000.00 with one school.

Only a contracted vendor can receive contracts above $25,000.00. After calming down the party going on within, I realized the potential for growth this would have for my company. Once I did an amazing job with her young leaders, the word was going to spread. Her business manager explained to me how to put together a work order. I emailed her that work order and invoice for $24,168.80 and explained why I could not receive the whole $28k…but, she already knew why.

Before I left the meeting with the principal, she told me that when I first met with her, her secretary came into the office and told her a vendor was outside with flowers and candy. She immediately said it was not for her, that it must be for someone else. But her secretary had insisted that it was for her as if she knew, and that is what got me in. That is what pimping the situation looks like. How did a pop-up turn into a meeting that lasted a little over an hour? What was I offering, or selling rather, by which she was intrigued? Well, what I was there to sell her was my social emotional program I created from my curriculum called the P.A.S.A.L.E.S program.

Though I was there to sell a 78 session twice a week workshop, manual, workbook, and all for the entire school year, I presented it as an experience rather than a product. I expressed it cinematically by telling the origin of how I came to be in this position sitting before her. I sold who I had become. I sold the emotions of a young Black man from the ghetto of South Jamaica Queens trying to climb out of a hole. I sold the idea that if I had the mentoring and guidance this curriculum provides, I could have been a fortune 500 CEO. Yes, the flowers and candy got me in the door, but selling my experience is what kept me inside.

Elevator Pitch

Have you heard of the term elevator pitch? Whether you heard of it or not, it is imperative that you have one written and memorized. An elevator pitch is all about rhetoric. A brief and persuasive speech that you use to create interest in what you are doing as a business and brand. An elevator pitch should be no longer than 60 seconds. I advise striving for 35-45 seconds if you can.

Why is it important? Time, alongside water, is the most valuable resource we have as a human species. Having a great and prepared elevator pitch available means you can communicate the most important aspects of yourself and your business simplistically. The purpose of your pitch is to get to your point fast. In the chapter, "What Glitters is Not Always Gold," I talk about when I was given one-minute to pitch my services to a high school coordinator. Let us look at my elevator pitch again.

"I created a social emotional curriculum that teaches life lessons to build character and morale based on my life experiences equipped with a teacher's manual that allows me to spread my program amongst the country. Topics range from how to present yourself, how to effectively communicate, friendships and understanding relationships, fear, the art of listening, emotional intelligence, self-awareness, teamwork, the power of humility, and the mental struggle and significance of following your dreams, ending with chapter 10, triumph. I'm currently in *two middle schools in the Bronx, in negotiation with the Osborne organization to get me and my curriculum on Rikers Islands for the young men detained,* and *my mission is to be the person I wish I had growing up."*

And in just 38 seconds my pitch was said and it became what I did. There are four components I followed that are in my pitch: (1) define the problem/establish the need, (2) describe your solution, (3) know your target market and (4) describe the competition. On the next page will be a breakdown of these four components in this pitch.

1. **Define the problem/establish the need**: Last line, "my mission is to be the person I wish I had growing up." The problem: The need for more Black men with troubled pasts and life experiences as teachers. To mentor and guide our young scholars' minds and energy with exercises and activities of reality to help with their understanding of who they are in this world and know that they have help. To be culturally self-sufficient and aware.

2. **Describe the solution**: For our young scholars to believe in something they must be able to see it. I represent for them the success that is obtained from changing your life around from making a ton of bad decisions and having life smack you around with its cold hands. I have a winning story for a Black man in America. I am the result. Which mostly came from mentorship, which is a huge part of my overall narrative. As well as good ole fashion luck. But those

opportunities arose only when I was prepared for it, you summon your blessings.
3. **Know your target market**: Second sentence from last line: "…two Middle schools in the Bronx… Osbourne Organization … Rikers Island." Clearly my services are for the youth who may have been detained and for those I am helping to avoid from being detained.
4. **Describe the competition**: The competition for me in my field is the lack of Black men with troubled pasts who turned their lives around teaching. We need more Black men with life experiences to help with moving our young scholars forward. My competition would be the system. And there is a lack of supply for this known demand in the Black educational community. There needs to be more community involvement.

The number one key factor in my success and for yours will be the consistency of your pitch. Since day one my pitch has been strong. Knowing who you are and being able to talk about yourself and what you do confidently unconsciously forms your pitch. When you add structure to it, like these four components, you give it purpose. It's a strategy to a plan and it starts with: if you had thirty seconds in an elevator with someone who could position you where you want to be in life, what would you say to them? Really think about it on your own time and create one. It really helps.

The Power of Self-talk and Visualization

You know that voice in your head? That is God. Not the God you may think, but you, God. It is your voice. You are the universe wrapped in flesh. Everything you do in life that manifests in this physical world comes from the things you tell yourself. I popped up at that school with flowers and candy knowing I was going to meet someone that could lead me further than where I was then.

Any step closer is a win. So even if I had gone into the school, having left only my package behind with someone who could decide whether or not to work with me, and had not seen the Principal, I cannot look at that as a failure. That negative thought becomes an emotion and would have triggered depression, minimized my energy to pursue, and fed inaction. Instead, I look at moments like that positively, since it makes me one step closer than I was before I walked in the building.

For every bad thought you have, counter it with two positive thoughts. If something bad does happen, think about how far you came, how blessed you are, and what you have as opposed to what you do not. I know there is a process I have to trust, and I never take no's personal. I know what I have to offer is the bomb.

LOVE YOURSELF

You must trust your product because you're your product. Also understand this, every time you think, you pray. If you do not want it in your life do not think about it. Because the devil will tell you a lie in your own voice.

You must always be your number one fan and supporter and know that emotions are contagious. You ever wondered why you started laughing just from watching someone else laugh, and you do not even know the joke. Or started crying because the other person was crying or giving off a sad emotion? The answer is because emotions are contagious. So just imagine if you believe in your product what the results would be. Yes, people will believe in it too. You must believe in yourself and this belief must be felt once you walk in the room. And it all begins with the things you tell yourself. With how positive your self-talk is, not just in the moment, but after as well. You must always remain positive and optimistic even if the deal falls through. The only thing permanent in life is death and nothing is personal. It took me years for that "it's not personal" comprehension. But like the great Sri Sri Ravi Shankar once said, **"Nothing in the world can bother you as much as your own mind… In fact, others seem to be bothering you, but it is not others, it is your mind. The primary cause of unhappiness is never the situation but your thoughts about it."**

While writing my workbook, negative self-talk would cripple me for weeks. I'd tell myself, "Who in the world do you think you are trying to write a curriculum based on your life experiences to get implemented into the white man's system? And how are you going to get the Department of Education, who follows the same format the factory owners structured in the 1800s, to believe in a young Black brother from South Jamaica Queens? How are you going to pull this off?" That right there is negative self-talk. It triggers my insecurities causing me to be depressed and inactive. If it was not for me understanding the process that comes with writing and knowing that what comes with pursuing projects could span months into years, I would have given up.

If I had not thought back to how interested and inspired the kids were at the career days I attended to serve as inspiration, I would have given up. If I had not countered every bad thought with a positive one, I would have given up. Self-Talk and visualization are real things and will determine your actions. It is imperative that you see yourself winning.

After securing $24,168.80, my biggest account to date, I decided to go to two more schools in the district. One I had worked with the prior year and the other was on the list I received from Darren's connection within the district. I walked into all schools unannounced because no one returns emails or follows up on phone calls. Plus, showing up in person applies pressure and that can do a lot for you.

The second school on my list was a ten-minute walk away. I walked through the doors up to the desk to sign in. I handed over my ID to the school safety guard as she penned me in and who turned the corner? The Assistant Principal.

"Hey Mr. Wray, give me a minute. I'll tell the principal you're here." "Thank you, Sir."

"Here you go Sir. Sign your name here please." I took my ID from the safety guard and signed in. I waited for the Assistant Principal in the main office. Five minutes later he comes out and says, "Walk with me…" so we started walking towards his office.

"You have an invoice on you," he asks. "No, but I can find one in my emails."

I go through my emails to his school and find the last email I had prepared. We printed it up and headed back to the main office where the principal's office was located.

"Sit right here, I'll call for you." He went into the principal's office with the invoice. I took a deep breath and sat patiently. Two minutes later he called me into the office. I shook hands with the principal and took my seat.

"Mr. Wray, I've been told wonderful things about your program. Can you fill me in a little more?"

"The P.A.S.A.L.E.S program covers the entire school with the goal of building a relationship with your students where I teach them life lessons, personal and social awareness and how I monetized my talent and turned my transgressions into an asset. My primary goal is to be for them the person I wish I had growing up. I also have connections with the New York Knicks and will bring in someone to speak to the kids. I have a college preparatory tour in June where I offer a wide variety of activities and experiences that build character and morale."

"Sounds good. Okay, so, put together an invoice for…." She leaned down to her laptop seemingly going through her budget to see how much she had available.

"Okay Mr. Wray. Make an invoice for $20,000 dollars and have it for me by tomorrow. The deadline to have this in is Friday, so please, get it to me ASAP." "Will do."

"I look forward to working with you Mr. Wray."

"Likewise. Thank you."

I got up, shook her and the Assistant Principal's hands, and headed out the office. Before I could make it to the front desk, I began to feel the alcohol burn in my nose because I was about to tear up. I had just made $44,128.80 in less than two hours. I thought, "this is not happening right now." Unbelievable. And I still had one more school to go. I left and walked seventeen minutes to the third school on my list.

I was confident, not only because this school was in the same district as the other two but also it was a school referred to me from the first school I had worked with. So what was I doing as I walked to this school? I envisioned myself winning. I told myself that I got the account already; I was just going to confirm.

I arrived at the school, signed in, and was directed to the main office on the second floor. The principal had just finished making his midday rounds. After introducing myself and who I was referred by, he informed me that he had already spent his funding, but that I should go to the middle school downstairs on the first floor. He told me was not sure if they found a vendor yet, but he knew they had received the same funding.

I went downstairs, walked into the main office, and asked to speak to the principal who was standing in front of me on the opposite side of the aisle. He seemed a little tense. He heard me tell his secretary who I was and why I was there. 30 seconds later he waved me into his office and told me I only had a few minutes. Well, those few minutes became almost two hours.

His Assistant Principal would join us only minutes into my pitch and boy, did I sell it. We got so personal I was able to learn that his Assistant Principal and I shared the same birthday. As I was talking to his Assistant Principal the Principal was skimming through my workbook. He could not hold back his admiration for the topics.

"And you did this all by yourself," he asked.

"Yes Sir. Took me nearly two years to write."

"Now this is what we need in schools regularly. I have been listening to you and I want to work with you. But the only thing I ask you is this, I want you to produce a trip where you can take my students, so they can experience the lessons you are teaching. If you are talking about humility and the art of listening, take them somewhere where they can experience it as well."

He got up and went to his computer. Then he got on his phone and called who I came to learn was his business manager asking where he put the $28,000 dollars because he chopped it up not expecting to spend it. Not expecting me to walk through the door with a program that fits the criteria, he sent the funding to other places to be spent.

After about eight minutes, he told me to put together an invoice for $20,000 dollars for the program. I agreed to everything and told him I would have it for him the next day. After the meeting I walked out like I just left a family barbecue. I walked towards the D train in complete awe. All three schools I went to I got. I never made this much money doing anything, legal or illegal. I called my brother immediately.

"Bro guess what?" I took a deep sigh

"What's up?"

"I just left my third school for the day and they all want me to send them invoices. Guess how much the total is?"

"What?"

"Bro, I just made $64,128.80 within a three-hour window."

"Stop lying."

"Dead-ass."

"Wow. You are doing it. You are fucking doing it bro. You called it too. You said 2018 was going to be the year. I am happy for you."

"Thanks. I had to tell somebody; this is crazy.

"So, what are you about to do now?

"Hop on this D train coming, go to Applebee's and have a few drinks."

"Okay, cool. Proud of bro. Keep pushing."

"Thanks brother. Later."

"Later."

I would be lying to you if I say a negative thought does not creep into my mind every now and again. I would not be a real entrepreneur if I had no anxiety or depression at times. I am human. It is going to happen. It is when you let the negativity win and define your purpose that matters. It is okay to feel sad or down or unmotivated and uninspired at times. Just do not stay there.

All that I have accomplished is because I tell myself I am great. I am worthy. I got this. I was born for this. I know my success begins with the conversations I have with myself. It begins with my power to suffocate distractions and stay focused. One of the distractions I try to avoid is the criticism I receive from my kids' mother for putting my dreams before our kids. Yes, it is a distraction. But I am willing to deal with the criticism of not being shit in the moment, to save the old bitter person I will become tomorrow if I do not get this done. I can change how I am viewed with time, what I cannot fix are my regrets. You must be able to live with inadvertently hurting the feelings of those you love, to further sustain the suffocation of distractions to achieve your goals. And this all begins with what you tell yourself.

I know that last part about my kids' mother came out of nowhere, but that day of signing up with three schools, made all the time I do not get to spend with my kids worth it. Sometimes we beat ourselves up because we allow others to make us feel bad for seeing the bigger picture. Everything I ever accomplished as a business is because of what I tell myself and what I see in my head. I visualize the reality I want to happen and it happens. I tell myself I got it and I go after it. This is the power of self-talk and visualization.

LOVE YOURSELF

On a scale of 1 to 10, with one meaning "not confident" and 10 meaning "very confident," how confident are you moving forward in life? (Circle your answer)

1   2   3   4   5   6   7   8   9   10

On a scale of 1 to 10, with one meaning "not confident" and 10 meaning "very confident," how positive is your self-talk? (Circle your answer)

1   2   3   4   5   6   7   8   9   10

I am curious, for question 1, why wasn't your answer higher?

_____

_____

_____

_____

For question 2, why wasn't your answer higher?

_____

_____

_____

_____

What negative self-talk do you tell yourself that holds you back? What are you blaming or using to justify the reason you do not act?

_____

_____

_____

_____

_____

_____

Now write down what you are going to do to reach and stay at a 10.

_____

_____

_____

_____

_____

_____

LOVE YOURSELF

I KNOW THIS IS RANDOM, BUT I WANT TO SHARE THIS..

I know a lot of men who do not have a good relationship with their childrens' mother at all. For most of us we were kids having kids. We became the images we had seen in our childhood. The behavior reflected in our community. Without the proper boots for the storm, we ended up trampling in the same puddles.

To completely hate someone we used to smile with, eat with, and share our bodies with is an issue we have within ourselves. Holding onto hate, making it difficult for peace. So much so that we become comfortable in this hate for one another, not realizing that it affects YOU. It affects HIM or HER. It affects the KIDS.

I understand that everyone's situation is different. It is easy to say screw someone and not deal with them ever again if there is no reason to be connected. But with a person you must deal with for the rest of your life, you have to be on good terms.

When your child or children speak about their parents it should be in a positive light as a union, not just as individuals. Because even if separated you will always be a family. Our children should have the proper model to follow, so they can know what to expect. I know this is all easier said than done, but we do not want our kids to think that hating either of their parents is the way it is supposed to be.

It says a lot about us as parents in our kids' eyes that, at least for them, we are able to keep things cordial. That we have the MATURITY and RESPECT to not make it about us. Because at the end of the day, it makes my relationship better with my kids when me and my kids' mother are good.

It makes life with that special person I am with better when me and my childrens' mother's issues are resolved and we RESPECT one another. To be 40 years old and hating the person who gave our kids life is immature and unhealthy. I know it is hard, sometimes the holes in the wall cannot be spackled. And who has time to completely knock it down and put one back up when the love isn't there anymore? In most cases when the damage is deeply done, a third party is needed for reconciliation. For many, it is an impossible feat to reconcile. I get that. And if you feel that way, at least pass the wisdom on to your children, a man, woman, or couple who may benefit from what it is supposed to be.

The only way we save our future and our community, is if we make a better place for the generation after us. It all begins with loving you and it all begins with a loving family. Please try to be the example of what love is supposed to be. Remember, before the drama, before the blocking of the phone calls, the fighting, the defamation of character, before the courts and other people were involved, there was a time when you two lived. When you two laughed. When you two loved, and everything was all good.

I respect the mother of my children because she knew how important pursuing my destiny was to me and did not make it difficult. She allowed me to pursue my dreams because she understands the legacy I want to leave behind.

If you do not have any kids yet, do not have any if you are not where you want to be in your life. Your situation may not be like mine where the opposite parent understands. To many, I may come off as a selfish prick for not putting my kids first. But I do not care about other people's opinions. To me, I *am* putting them first.

Bitter old people with regrets tend to blame anyone they can for why they could not pursue their dreams. I will never forget the day my mother told me she could not continue her education because she had to raise us three ungrateful bastards (her exact words by the way).

LOVE YOURSELF

A toxic mother who does not want her kids is far worse than an absent father. I am exactly like my mother and it took me having two kids of my own to understand why she felt the way she did. Therefore, I would rather be criticized for being a half-ass dad now because I can change how I am viewed in time by stepping up. Especially since they are still young. What I will not be able to change is any regrets I may have for not going all in in pursuing my dreams.

What is fear?

There are two types of fear. The state of fear and the trait of fear. In his book, *The Fearless Executive*, Alan Downs speaks about the trait of fear being an imagined catastrophe, an avoidance of social interaction. Being afraid to take risks because of an outcome that is not connected to any present danger.

While the state of fear is an unexpected danger, walking through a graveyard at night or through the projects in the ghetto, all constitute the state of fear. Unknown and unexpected, but present.

I believe that many are born with a by-any-means-necessary attitude. From robbing people to get money to selling drugs to survive, I took every chance I could to get money and make my dream a reality. I did not care what I did to get there, that is how badly I wanted it. It was more important than my freedom. I had no fear. And that is the same mentality you must have for life in general. You must be fearless.

You must be willing to die to live, but it must be focused on the positive realm because there are manufactured laws one must follow. My fearlessness was also cultivated. You cannot fear jail when you have been in jail. You cannot be scared and worried about being homeless when you have been homeless. You cannot fear death when you have faced it. Having no choice really matters.

I turned my greatest fear into fuel. Even if you do not know what you want to do, let who you do not want to become be enough motivation and inspiration you need to get the job done. Remove the fear and you will remove the chains that keep you shackled. Everything begins and ends with how you think, view, and interpret things. Fear is real. We all as humans can relate to it. But how it affects your actions is up to you. For fear only attracts the very thing you are trying to avoid. The only way to develop courage is to embrace your fears. Do what makes you uncomfortable.

Do what scares you. There is no bad that can come from it. Only a newer braver version of you. I wrote my first book out of fear of not becoming the man I knew I had the talent to become. I used fear as motivation. I view every situation positively and because I trained my mind to see the good in the bad, I no longer believe in bad situations.

Here is an example: instead of looking at my incarceration as a negative thing, I focused my concentration on the positive of the situation and that was the time I had to become better. To study my craft and understand where I went wrong. I used this time to become a better person. If I allowed the perception of my situation and opinion of society, who views me as a criminal, then nothing good would have come of those three years and I would have continued to attract negative things.

There are no mistakes in life, only lessons. Any struggle you will go through is just a test to see if you are deeply committed to the life you say you want. You will question your purpose, but know that nothing is a setback. It is all a part of the process of achieving knowledge of self so that you can get out of your own way.

Your unhappiness is because you are not in alignment with who you are. You are fighting your authenticity. You are fighting your standards and what you believe in. That is why you are always arguing with your mate. Why your job makes you miserable. Why you cannot seem to have a consistent flow of happiness. You will never escape your heart. You have a choice, you either listen or you do not. Oprah Winfrey said, *"Every right decision I have ever made has come from my gut. Every wrong decision I've made was the result of me not listening to the greater voice of myself."*

Get out of that shitty relationship you keep making excuses for. Quit that job that has no ladder. So what the money is good, your happiness is more important. I know it is not as simple as it reads, but nonetheless it is a choice. A choice that determines whether you live or simply exist. A choice that comes with grave consequences. Be mindful of this, the price of inaction is far greater than the cost of a mistake.

You must figure out what debt you are willing to die with.

Read aloud: All things are possible if I believe in myself a little more. If I go the extra mile. If I push past the pain. If I face my fears and have the courage to endure. To embrace the humility of knowing that a greater force exists, not only from what my eyes can see, but exists within me. I am a part of a natural order too deep to fully comprehend, but a part of it nonetheless, which means that I am great.

Keep dreaming, even if it breaks your heart

Following who you know you are and what you know you can do fearlessly will lead you down roads where hitchhikers fear. Asking for a ride with no destination but your inaction in mind, will have you thinking that you are traveling the wrong path. There will be detour signs that create the illusion of a safer, more secure destination, but you must stay on your path, no matter how scary it seems.

I never stopped writing, it just led into something more than music. I was told numerous times I suck, to not quit my day job, "this is not for you." What if I gave up? If I allowed my broken heart of not becoming a recording artist to keep me down, you would not be reading this book right now. Though my powers are being exploited on an unexpected platform, I am still doing what I love to do, and that is write.

There are life lessons you must learn in the pursuit of dreams that can only come from making mistake after mistake after mistake. After letdown after letdown after letdown, you will be knocked down and discouraged, yes. But if you keep dreaming, keep vibrating as your authentic self, exercising these laws even when it seems too far to reach, you will get there. It took me what seemed like forever to be walking in my purpose, but I am walking in it because I kept dreaming even when it broke my heart.

Following your dreams and being fearless in your pursuit will be the hardest act to do, but never second guess your gut. There is no timetable. Age is just a number. It's not that if I do not have a house or a car by 25 or 35 I am a failure. The last thing you want to do is accumulate debt and to have too many expenses at an early age. A lot of successful people did not make it big until later in their lives.

Also, there is a saying floating around about waiting your turn. That one must be patient. Well, there is a stark difference between being patient and wasting time. You do not wait your turn, you *make* your turn. Those who wait only get the scraps left behind by those who choose to hustle and be fearless, over being content and complacent.

If it doesn't scare you just as much as it excites you, if you're not nervous and becoming self-conscious and questioning what the hell you're doing the next day after you just called yourself a genius, if you have never been on the brink of giving up, then you need to reevaluate the reason you're doing this all for. Because nothing worth having has given an easy fight.

If you do not think about quitting, you are not playing hard enough. It may not be where you want to be, but it will always be where the universe needs you the most. I wanted to be a lawyer in high school and a rapper in my early 20s. Truthfully, I really thought I would be a multi-platinum recording artist and songwriter by now. But that is just not where I am needed at this time, and frankly, I do not have the passion for it anymore. But it was the fact that I pursued both these dreams that led me to where I am now. Remember, your purpose has nothing to do with you and everything to do with being in the service of others.

LOVE YOURSELF

What do lawyers do? They defend the truth. What am I doing now as a mentor, author, and curriculum developer? I am defending my truth. What do rappers do? Rappers perform on stage for an audience. The Department of Education is my stage and the kids are my audience. So I might not technically be a lawyer or a rapper, but my duties are the same. Therefore, it is important to follow your dreams no matter what because dreams lead to purpose.

On the next page is the F.I.G tree. Questions I answered with complete honesty to motivate you to do the same. I will never ask you for something I am not willing to give myself. We all deal with fear, insecurities, and guilt. Let your answer reflect what you read here in Part 2. Here is my truth:

THE F.I.G TREE

What do you *fear*?
JAMAI: I used to fear that I would not be taken seriously because I did not have a degree in Education and Curriculum Development. That this lack of credentials would hold me back from having any success. That I would be viewed as a scam artist. I was afraid that my past would somehow hurt my future.

What are you *insecure* about?
JAMAI: My teeth. My smile.

What do you feel *guilty* about?
JAMAI: I used to feel guilty for not making my kids my number one priority. I would beat myself up about instructing other kids more than I was teaching my own.

THE F.I.G TREE

Based on what you *Fear* the most, what do you allow to distract you?

_____

_____

_____

_____

Based on what you are *Insecure* about, why do you think you continue to allow these distractions to suffocate your focus?

_____

_____

_____

_____

What do you feel *Guilty* about?

_____

_____

_____

_____

Universal Laws

How to understand and better how you are using…

- The law of intention,
- The law of Inspired Action,
- and the spiritual law of manifestation.

LAW OF INTENTION

The universal law states that intentions are much more powerful than wants, wishes, or hopes. Intention releases a force that makes things happen. Whatever your aim in life, if you gather the energy and keep your target in sight, the force of the Universe backs your vision. That is the power of intention. Intention is taken into consideration when assessing karma. When your intentions are noble and honorable, even if your plan does not come to fruition, you will be rewarded for the purity of your ideals. It is the intention that signals the rightness (or otherwise) of an idea or project. Make sure that your intentions do not come from the ego but are for the highest good as

Universal energy supports the highest good. It is the basis of manifestations.

— Joanne Walmsley, Sacred Scribes

Remember the story I told you about Mr. Magic wanting me to write my story down? How he wanted me to meticulously write down every achievement, every house I plan to own, every movie and play I plan to write. How many kids I plan to have, cars I want to own, down to the kind of woman I see myself with.

What he was letting me know without saying it is that your magnet of attracting what you desire becomes stronger when you put it on paper. It makes it a reality because it exists and can be seen not just in your mind, but now with your eyes.

Write down what you intend to do. Feel it in your bones. Intentions have just as much energy as actions.

Now let me show you something. I was scrolling through IG yesterday and came across something that said, *"sometimes it takes ten years to get that one year that will change your life. Keep going."* Going through some of my notes from when I was incarcerated, I unearthed some ideas that I had written down on businesses I wanted to own and things I wanted to do.

I wrote this list down on January 2, 2007. I kid you not, I said I was going to write a self-help book titled, *My Self-help Book*, and that it would be a combination of all the books I read, all my experiences, mistakes, and wisdom I'd obtained up to that point.

At this time I was only 26, but I swore I knew it all like all young adults full of pride do in their twenties. I totally forgot I wrote this down. I forgot I even mentioned anything about being an author because I was heavy into music at that time. I started writing the book you are reading now on August 27th, 2017, ten years later. Now how crazy is that?

LOVE YOURSELF

The photo on the next page has the date I wrote the list. The following pages are the things I wanted to accomplish as an entrepreneur and as a brand. Honestly, I totally forgot I wrote this list. The conscious mind, which is responsible for memory, tends to forget. But the subconscious mind, which is much more powerful, holds all that ever was and will ever be and is where manifestation begins.

1. Take $100,000 and build studio.
   - Hire engineers and producers to mix and master and produce tracks.
   - Sit down with a lawyer (Entertainment) and structure your label. Contracts, trademarks, logos etc. Make sure all legal work is taking care of becoming making any more. (Have legal work done before putting out any music, or shopping your lyrics to a label as a songwriter.)
   - Refer to Starting an Independent Record label for guidance.
   - Set up corporate account for M Wray Records as well.

* M Wray Greetings, Records, Publishing, Shoes and Apparel, and Wray of light Productions will all be subsidiaries under the M Wray Enterprise umbrella.

Business #3 - M Wray Publishing ...

Note: M Wray Greetings will be the first company started followed by Records and then Publishing. When Greetings is secure and all the basic hard work like technical firms, Manufacturing and Marketing is done where Profit starts come. Then focus goes to Records and Publishing. Records first.

Books
1. Black Agent? The Story of Carolina Slim (Finished)
2. My Self-help Book
3. My life.
4. Continue Black Agent? Series
5. Acquire Authors under the imprint
6. Write a book about my life and career until the end of my vision. Before it actually happens. Then for the 2nd book, years later when most of everything is accomplished, write what made it come true. Publish the 1st one sooner. dates 1980-2040.

Lady Wray Lagarre

First Thing First — Business #1 - M Wray Greetings ~~bank~~ which will be the method ①

1. Start M Wray Greetings (Lawyers, Trademark, sole proprietorship, Tax I D#, Corporate Account)
   - Take proof of existence of the corporation to bank of choice and open an corporate account.
   - Take whatever money, not all, maybe, and put in this corporate open account.

* Prior to this sit down with lawyer with a couple hundred dollars and create corporation.
   - After corporation is up, money is in corporate account, the money that you will leave in your personal savings account $1,000,000⁺ is the money you need to show the bank you have the capital to pay back the $1,000,000 dollar loan your taking out to fund your business.

* After money is where it needs to be, both corporate and personal accounts, take out a $1,000,000 dollar loan to finance M Wray Greetings. Now your credit won't be good enough, that's why you need money ($1 million plus) to show you have the capital to pay the loan back. Which, in the end, boosts your credit through the roof.

* The reason why you want the majority, not all, your money in a corporate account is because monies in a corporate account gains 25% interest. Meaning $250,000 off of every $million dollars. Now that $250,000 is taxed at about $40,000 est. You can even give it the IRS or donate it to a charitable donation or family member on welfare/in need.

Note: Just as long as your taking action in starting the company so you can make a profit before the 3, maybe 5 year period is up, your good.
   - Start off as an sole proprietorship, as company grows, sell stocks. Just make sure that you always have 51%. Whatever you sell the stocks for that money is yours to do whatever. Just at the end of the year however much % age a stockholder holds is what he gets of the profit annually.

As far as M Wray Greetings, go to patent lawyers to patent idea first, once idea is patent, or patent is pending go to the technical firm to make prototype. Then, find a manufacter to manufacture invention and start to Market, Promote, and Advertise to the country/world.

Put this AS INTRODUCTION to my book which will be the collaboration of all the books I've written out of on paper during by bid Make sure to put glossary in back for the words (big words) especially from What is a man?

Introduction — From U.S. News and World Report • Dec 31, 07/Jan 7, 08

The more you read, the greater likelihood that you will do well in school, be successful in business, and become involved in your community. More than income, social class, or education, NEA Chairman Dana Gioia says "Reading allows us to achieve more of our personal potential than almost any other activity."

Tufts University Child Development Prof. Maryanne Wolfe says "Reading not only creates its own circuitry within the brain, that circuitry gives us the capacity to go beyond the text to new thoughts of our own." She goes on to say, "My worry is that our children and our societal immersion into the ever more immediate, digital presentational format for text will short-circuit" part of that ability. The antidote; Read on.

Direct   Take Time To Listen. Don't jump, even though tempted, in before the other
Quote   person finishes speaking. Stop interrupting. It's rude, selfish, and shows lack of
From   discipline as well as the care for what the other has to say. If you let them finish, what
US News   you're dying to say or jump in with you might not have to say once they finish.

If you hear only the words without paying attention to the speaker's tone of voice, facial expressions, and body language, you risk missing nuanced, underlying meanings or important signals. Confirm you're understood: A concise paraphrase will acknowledge that you're gettin' the message. And when it's your turn to speak, know you've provided a model for how you hope your words will be received.

Attentiveness and understanding - the qualities that differentiate physically hearing from actually listening — can be hard to cultivate. Learn to take in more clearly and you'll enhance your personal and professional skill sets alike. "Business is all about relationships, and being a better listener helps you establish more positive relationships"

" Those who do not know their opponents' arguments do not completely understand their own."
" It is better to debate a question without settling it than to settle a question w/o debating it"
                                                                    — Joseph Joubert (1754-54)

Here is me structuring this self-help book.

Intro: This is not an attempt to show you how to start and run a Fortune 500 company but it attempt to stir you from making the same mistakes I did and how to turn what perceives to be bad into some good. How I came home from prison and made a stand to love myself, respect myself, and accomplish the goals I set while incarcerated.

My Self-Help Book — Based from Observation, experience, and education

"Strength is in Numbers" — But that doesn't mean become a gang member and surround yourself with people that's not going to uplift you and help you see and utilize your strengths and individual talents. Which leads me to

Textbook Knowledge vs Knowledge of Self

You can have all the quotes, sciences, formulas, philosophies, knowledge and information from thousands of books. But if you don't know who you "have knowledge of yourself," then how would the application of this knowledge (information) you read and seem to memorize be instrumental in the betterment of you as an individual if what you claim to know, which sounds good and convincing, doesn't focus on you as a person. Knowing your likes and dislikes, separating what you know you need from what you think you want. How can you adopt someone else's opinion as your own just because it correlates with what you believe in, then you're still not sure what you believe in? When you still are having an identity crisis, suppressing your personality (which we'll talk about later) because your textbook knowledge supersedes the knowledge of yourself. The best knowledge to have is the knowledge of self. And at the same time "Having knowledge doesn't mean you're smart, it's the application of that knowledge that shows your intelligence."

How to Obtain Knowledge of Self

First you must release your fear of the unknown. Why? Because knowing who you are, includes having experiences under your belt. Sure trial and error. So, being scared of not knowing the outcome, when it pertains to positive lifestyle is only stagnated your growth.

★ Do not read and learn things to make people feel inferior. A true Growth/man looking can walk into a crowd of people and be an expert on their topic but you still never know it all so, Never flaunt what you think you know. Genius in one of the knowledge out there is solely for educational purposes. Which leads to the Unwanted Material. Material that's not pertinent/relevant to anything prosperous.

Correlating Chapters
Fear — Unwanted Material
Action — Like Minds attract
Suppressed Personality
Understanding

God does not know what's good or bad because God is not a man. Everything good, bad, evil, all the demons, devils, and angels all comes from man. All the suffering, war, death, and disease is created by man. Have you ever questioned why God lets innocent people die? You ever ask why God allows poverty and evil to rule the Earth?

Do you think praising Him and following the commandments is going to get you into what you call heaven? No. It does not work that way. All souls are saved. Everything you believe in when it comes to religion is man and his ego. You will not remember your time on Earth. Not even a little bit of it.

Think about it, you live all your life trying to get into heaven, but when you die you will not even know if you got into heaven and whether or not all you did was worth it because all is erased. And that is the greatest trick religion plays on man. Searching for his peace outside of himself and putting his peace into the hands of another.

Every law I broke was because I was either hungry or because I believed it would get me closer to what I desired. Every unwise decision I made to achieve my goals always had the right intention because I was always chasing the life my talent could produce. I was always trying to manifest what I desired. The reason it took me so long to get here is because I was breaking the laws of man.

Stealing is a crime. A law of man. That crime…my actions, put me behind bars. But my intentions were to be who I wanted to be. These intentions and desires were connected to my authentic self.

I was going to get to this level of achievement regardless because my intentions were always right, it was just my actions in breaking the law that caused the delay. What is a crime? What is illegal? Alcohol was illegal at one time, now it's legal.

Marijuana was illegal at one time, now it is legal. Going back hundreds of years ago, raping and killings and many other horrendous acts was a norm and was not against the law. It may have not been morally correct, I am not saying it is right by any stretch of the imagination, but it was not a crime.

Tax is a crime. What the pharmaceutical companies are doing to us is a crime. Police killing unarmed men is a crime. Putting harmful chemicals in our food to kill us is a crime. There are millions of crimes committed day by day by the very people that make the law. I'm not saying this to justify my actions because I still believe you cannot serve two Gods. You cannot want sunshine if your thoughts are cloudy. There must be a balance and this balance comes from vibrating in whole righteously.

The power of intent is just as powerful as your actions. Yes, I ended up behind bars because of committing a crime, but because of my intent, for every unwise decision good was found and put me on the path to reach this destination. Going to jail saved my life.

I do not feel guilty for putting myself first anymore because I know my intentions will always be more powerful than others' perception. I am no longer fearful of my past negatively affecting my future. The results, my success, accounts for that. I am now free.

LAW OF INSPIRED ACTION

This is where you get to manipulate energy and put into motion your intention. This is an important Universal Law that many Law of Attraction enthusiasts forget about. When you begin to play around with the emotional scale, and you can move yourself up a step at any given point in time, you will be able to explore the realm of intent. You are already using intent, of course, but you may not be using it to your best advantage. The Law of Inspired Action kicks in when you have deliberately formed an intent. Your enthusiasm and desire for the intent to translate into a tangible result causes you to act, the first step. When you do this and continue to do it toward the manifestation of your intent, Universal Laws are bound to work in your favor. A real-life example is when a seed is caused to germinate by temperature and soil conditions. The seed has the intent to germinate; a change (action/energy) in its environment causes germination to occur.

— Psychic Elements

There is not too much to say about the law of action because it is obvious. The number one important thing for manifestation is to follow thought and idea with action. You must understand that Rome was not built in a day and everything is a process. Stay in the moment and enjoy your small steps materializing. Stop overthinking and procrastinating.

The plan does not have to be perfect for you to act. The majority of success stories like my own had to be tweaked. But I would have never known what to tweak if I never acted. ACT NOW and early. If you are in your twenties, you can always bounce back. You do not want to be 40 years old getting into financial hardships and instability. The longer you wait to act, the more likely you are to give up. No one wants an old person chasing young people dreams.

LAW OF MANIFESTATION

The Spiritual law of Manifestation states that we manifest everything that comes into our lives. Everything in the Universe has an energetic frequency that is broadcasting on the etheric level. To bring to fruition and manifest in our lives the things we desire (no matter what they are) we must tune-in to its vibrational frequency… clarity is the key. Our thoughts, worries, and stresses send out interference, which stops us from fine-tuning to the frequency…be certain about exactly what it is that we want, otherwise we may receive something other than what we truly desire…picture it vividly.

Visualization is the most essential element. We must also have absolute faith that our intentions will come to fruition… If we want to attract a friend who is fun-loving, open-hearted, and genuine, then we must develop those qualities within ourselves. If we wish for a suitable partner, write down the exact qualities you wish for them to have. We must remember though, to possess those same qualities in return within ourselves. To engage the Spiritual Law of Manifestation focus on the higher qualities of what we are manifesting. "You are a living magnet. What you attract into your life is in harmony with your dominant thoughts."

– Brian Tracy

From the first time I held my book fresh off the press, to the career day with the kids, to the giving of 100 copies out to the youth, to making a workbook and curriculum from it, to currently teaching our future leaders, my actions have allowed me to manifest the life I wanted. To have reached here is the greatest feeling in the world. And for me, I have not even scratched the surface.

Before we leave here, I want you to write what you want from life. Write down the things you intend to do and have. It does not have to be entrepreneurial. It can be a degree you plan to get or a job and career you want to have. Everybody is not cut from the same entrepreneurial cloth. There would not be entrepreneurs if there were no employees. We all need each other. You are either a principal, teacher, or janitor. So, what do you want from life? What do you want your life to be? What do you see?

Part 3

The Branches:
Your Awakening

He who awakens can now see.

Paying attention to the signs

Are you seeing the same numbers when you look at the time? Does it feel like that billboard slogan is talking to you? Are you observing your negative patterns more? Your unhealthy diet? Are you more empathetic and compassionate? Has a single act produced events that you now understand you were destined to experience, even though you never saw it coming? Is your authenticity felt when you speak or walk into a room? Does it feel like the universe is arranging people, circumstances, and events to bring you closer to the reality you want for yourself?

If so, have you ever thought about why this is? Well, I have. And the reason behind it clearly revealed that I was moving towards a spiritual awakening. There are numerous signs. Spiritual awakenings often happen when your authenticity increases. When you are walking to your own beat. When you are being yourself in this world with no concerns about keeping up with the Joneses, pleasing others, and their opinions. You speak the truth and you share it with the world.

When you are awakening, ungoverned by instability and fear, the cancer around you begins to die and you disconnect from the toxicity and drama, no matter if they are close friends or relatives. You yearn for inner peace and will have it at any cost. But it gets deeper than just these signs. Numbers are the language of the universe.

LOVE YOURSELF

It started with my seeing the numbers 1127, 156 and 444. I understand now in retrospect that the moment it became about others and not me, the moment it was not about the material and money but instead about purpose and service, my life changed. I want to share with you the meanings of these three numbers. What you are about to read comes from a website by Joanne Walmsley, called Sacred Scribes Angel Number.

ANGEL #1127

"Angel Number 1127 is a message from your angels to maintain your positive attitude, outlook, and expectations, as these vibrations are manifesting abundance into your life. The Universal Spiritual Laws of Attraction, Abundance and Manifesting are working cohesively in your life and your angels want you to know that you are on the right life path and you are urged to continue. Do not fear the road ahead as it is filled with wonderful opportunities to grow and prosper on all levels. When you see the numbers of your date of birth repeating to you, it is often an indication that you are to concentrate and focus upon your true-life purpose..."

— Joanne Walmsley

ANGEL #156

"Angel Number 156 is a message from your angels that your material needs will be supplied as you start to make the necessary changes that you are prompted and guided

to make. Keep your thoughts positive and light, as your focus and attitude manifests and determines the realities of your life. The changes you need to make involve how you pursue, live, and serve your life purpose and soul mission. Angel Number 156 is a message that your determination to positively change your life (e.g., career, home, finances etc.) is being Divinely guided, so listen to your intuition and the guidance from the angels and pursue the course of action that takes you closer to living your personal truths. Your intuition is your link to the angels. Always be aware of angelic love as it is unconditional and always available."

— Joanne Walmsley

ANGEL # 444:

"444 is a clear sign from the Universe that you are exactly where you're supposed to be in this moment of your life. My advice to you? Trust your journey, trust the way your life unfolds, and trust that you are where you need to be at the present moment. In other words, 444 is your messenger telling you to have faith and be confident that things are going in the right direction in your life. Whenever you are seeing 444, the angels tell you that you are resonating with the Universe in perfect synchronicity."

— Joanne Walmsley

I had to know more. So, I got a numerology report done. What's numerology?

LOVE YOURSELF

NUMEROLOGY

Numerology is the study of numbers and their symbolism. These numbers will work as a guide so that things in your life are understood as you create the life you want. If you are experiencing seeing the same numbers, write them down and what you were thinking and/or talking about at the time. This will help you understand where you are in life and give you what you need to do or continue doing to fulfill your destiny.

I highly recommend getting your report done. It has helped me understand the truths about myself, both positives and negatives as well as things I was in denial about. How to make better choices and stop repeating the same destructive patterns of behavior.

Reading certain parts of my report lifted weight off my chest I did not know was there. I was completely blown away by how accurate it was, which is why I am going to connect parts of my report with events spoken about in this book to show how imperative it is to know this information about yourself.

Let us start with the month I was born. Better known as the formative cycle. The formative cycle begins at birth and ends at the beginning of 28 years of age.

Jamai, your Formative Cycle Number is eleven.

"Jamai, your Formative Cycle carries the vibration of the Master Number 11, which is sometimes called "the visionary." This is a difficult vibration for young people to handle, and whether due to the influence of adults or the advice of peers, it's possible that you withdrew from the exciting promise of 'a life less ordinary.' Having a good relationship with others

may have been more important to you than your inner gifts and dreams, and this could have made for a good deal of tension in your early years. However, everything changed during your teen years. Chances are good that you began to attract the inspiration to allow your inner gifts to flower, and the desire to do exceptional or unusual things. You are likely to have been drawn into a more intense and exciting lifestyle than the one you had previously established or had experiences that set you apart from your peers in some way."

The breakdown: "Visionary…" "a life less ordinary." Words that sound all so familiar when I think about my preteen and teenage years. Only thing is, I did not need any influence. The system of school, work, retirement, and death never made any sense to me. I always had a vision that undermined every example around me. Something my mother and I at that time could not come to terms with and a huge part of our early problems. The "getting along with others…" line especially resonates. I always tried to convince my peers to see what I saw. To want what I wanted. For years I carried that weight thinking I was not great and I did something wrong just for wanting more and being willing to do anything to get it. My way of thinking and ambition took me to places cultivating the man before you and the reason a lot of my friends that were, are not my friends now. Reading this at this point got my attention.

Jamai, your First Name Number is seven

"Because you have chosen to use a first name of the vibration Seven, Jamai, it is likely that you are

thought of by others as an expert, a deep thinker or a philosopher in some way, even when it's not voiced. They look for deeper or doubled meanings in what you have to say and will often expect you to be something other than an everyday person in a casual or social setting. Sometimes this misinterpretation of what you are "about" can disturb the social life unless you know many people of the same interests. You will have to fight the impression others may have that you are special, because that misperception can harm your relationships and your prosperity.

Make it clear that you are imaginative, and you will thrive in all situations. There is, however, a remedy—spend some time with a mirror staring into your own eyes and saying 'I trust you'—continue with this practice until you do, and you will see wonderful things happen in your life. Do not try to pretend that you are just like everyone else to get along; because it is your intelligence, expertise or insight that others are attracted to—and playing to it can be your strength.

The breakdown/connection: I read this quote a while ago that said, "when you're hanging around people who are not winning at life, talking about your accomplishments comes off like you're bragging." I experienced this in relationships and with family and friends. What always bothered me was that they knew my story. They knew that I had been chasing and living hard for 20+ years trying to bring my soul's work to the eye. They knew how hard it had been for me and it reflected in how I was living. You would think when I come with excitement about something I accomplished they would understand its pure joy. Finally, I am doing what I said I could do. If you are hanging around people who do not have the same ambition and wants from life, who do not hunger for things like you do, then you will always remind them of what they are not.

"… don't try to pretend that you're just like everyone else to get along; because it is your intelligence, expertise or insight that others are attracted to—and playing to it can be your strength…" I know two people who hate when I act humble and easygoing. They rather the cocky-confident-talk-his shit-Jamai. Which is who I am. Although I have learned that you must turn it on and off depending on the settings, they want to see that confidence. Because it is what gives them courage and hope in themselves. It powers them.

After reading that, I got really into the report. I was seeing myself.

Jamai, your Birthday number is nine

"This vibration favors expressing your experience to others; many opportunities to write, speak or teach are likely to be presented to you as well. Many people with this Birthday Vibration have a strong artistic side, which may be apparent in their lives, or may lay unexpressed, so if the opportunity to do so comes along, it would be best if you capitalized on it when it does. Just following along with social or political trends will not attract the kind of success that 'doing your own thing' will.

The breakdown/connection: That speaks for itself. Everything I was already doing.

My Life Path Number is 2.

"Jamai your Life Path is of the vibration Two. This path gives you the ability to work well with others and enables

you to thrive in any situation requiring joint effort or group participation. You also have an incredibly positive attitude. You are a natural negotiator and peacemaker. Chances are good that you have been called upon more than once to settle a disagreement or dispute between others. You are likely to have looked more than once at the possibility of becoming part of a spiritual path or discipline."

"You would prefer to help and serve rather than to lead, but this can be a negative trait sometimes. When you are under stress, you tend to become submissive rather than defensive, because of the tremendous emotional sensitivity you possess…"

"You tend to be more talkative than not, and you enjoy expressing yourself through singing, writing, acting, music, or some form of speaking. You may be known for the ability to turn an everyday conversation into a special experience, and you do not mind being in the spotlight from time to time. It's likely that you'll have a tendency towards extravagance though, and although you do well with creating wealth, you enjoy sharing it even more than you do making it."

"You may find that, from time to time, you can get lost in detail or need reassurance and approval from others, both of which can slow things down when trying to get the job done. People skills come naturally to you, and they can be your key to success in any field or activity you choose to pursue. In any disturbed atmosphere, Jamai, you can bring a touch of harmony through your gentle nature, your desire for balance, and your eye for beauty."

"Relationships are your top priority, because your natural drive seeks togetherness, rather than personal significance…Generally successful in matters of love, you will, on the whole, be happier in relationships than not, even if your partner does not meet your expectations. At the same time, this almost overwhelming desire to be accommodating, and cooperate, may leave you open to deception and disappointment."

"There are people who will take your kindness as vulnerability, rather than receive it with gratitude, and others may find the blind spot in your happiness, expecting you to comply with whatever demands they make or accept any excuses they give. Sometimes you may even prefer to be submissive and dependent rather than be alone—this is the dark side of your Life Path vibration."

"You can easily be carried away with your emotions sometimes, so it's important that you learn not to take things personally. This may cause oversensitivity and nervous tension, as well as the tendency to put yourself down, which blocks the intuitive ability. Sometimes, the ideas you attract may be way 'outside the box,' and this may cause you to wish it was easy for you to be more 'everyday' or practical. Try to unlearn that habit of thought, because it is your imagination and inspired, visionary way of thinking and being that people love about you. Denying your 'difference' and trying to live without your intuitive gifts will keep you from attracting the success you deserve."

"The fact that you are generally well liked is your redeeming quality because you will tend to attract people from all ends of the spectrum, and that includes trustworthy ones.

LOVE YOURSELF

Although your life favors marriage or other forms of committed partnership, friends are extremely important to you, and an important key to your happiness, prosperity and success."

Again, I was blown away by how accurate the report was. Of course you do not know me well enough to put all the pieces together, but trust me when I say that this was so spot on it was scary. This helped me to understand that if my decisions are aligned with my true self, with my true nature and essence, I will always feel uplifted and accomplished. Inspired and focused. And in the moment. Relax and truly listen to your thoughts and feelings. Please get this done for yourself. It is key to loving yourself. To know yourself is to love yourself. Let us move forward.

All quotes from this chapter in bold are all from my numerology report from www.numerlogist.com

THE F.I.G TREE

For this F.I.G tree, I wanted to pull from what I learned from "My Life Path Is Number 2" to answer what I feared, was insecure about, and felt guilty about. But at this point, there is not anything I am insecure or feel guilty about.

What do you *fear*?
JAMAI: I fear that because relationships are my top priority, that I will do the same thing in a new relationship that I did in my previous and put the relationship before purpose. That I will not listen to my true self. That I would love someone so much, even though they do not meet my expectations, and sacrifice my happiness and deceive myself again.

Please, go to www.numerologists.com to get your chart done today. It's worth it.

Universal laws

How to understand and better how you are using…

- The law of Attraction

LAW OF ATTRACTION

"The law of attraction is the belief that positive or negative thoughts bring positive or negative experiences into a person's life. The belief is based on the ideas that people and their thoughts are made from 'pure energy,' and that a process of like energy attracting like energy exists through which a person can improve their health, wealth, and personal relationships."

— Unknown Author

All of your reality, both good and bad, has been created by the energy you give off. I have attracted the success and love in the world I live in because I started with the root. Believed, detached, and forgave. I put purpose before a relationship and began the journey of loving myself. I healed. I changed my intent, acted, and what manifested is where I am now. Why? Based on the principle and law of attraction. It is quite that simple. Attract your world.

Visualization is also a huge part of attracting your desires. Every account I receive from schools I saw myself obtaining. I walked inside every school already with the vision in my head of me winning. That vision and confidence is felt in my energy and becomes contagious. Another especially important aspect of the law of attraction is being thankful for waking up. Being thankful to walk, talk, and use your arms.

Train your mind to always be thankful for what you have. To have your mind on what you lack only keeps you from what you want. Again, the universe does not know your intent, only what you say to yourself. After a while, when you realize that there are no bad situations, that there is no such thing as failure, things always go your way.

So much so that people will call you lucky. It is not that you are lucky, you just do not have negativity clouding your energy and the opportunities you receive are because you were prepared for it. People never see the work, only the results. Act and move as if you have it already. Be a walking magnet.

Part 4

The leaves: Loving Again

Before you ever get the person you really want in your life, you will be tested with every person that was wrong for you. You will be tempted with what was easy, what was familiar, what was only physical, what was safe and what was simply a friend to pull you out of a difficult situation because you did not want to be alone. When you finally meet the person you were meant to be with you will not have to guess, decide, or choose. You will be drawn to them. They will seem to fit who you are, but at the same time, you have the missing pieces that make you want to become a better person. There is no need to be guarded because this soul is like your own and talking to them about the deepest things in life is effortless. They will not be like any other you have met, and you will find yourself looking for parts of them in everyone you meet.

— Shannon L. Alder

Loving Again, but first...

After my breakup there were some things I had to come to terms with. It took a year for me to get to this place of understanding, but it was understanding these terms that began my healing process. The same way I had to forgive my mother, I had to forgive myself and my ex and understand that the three years we were together was not a waste of time. That this breakup was necessary for my evolution.

We all enter relationships with the idea that this person has the potential to be the one. Rarely does one look at the person they are getting involved with as just passing through. That their only purpose is to open your eyes to the toxicity and dysfunction we are blind to in ourselves. So, the first thing I had to do was forgive myself for holding on too long. I knew nine months into that relationship that it was not going to last, but I held on because I thought in time, I could change her. And later, I beat myself up for that.

I had to forgive her for the lies and betrayal. I had to forgive her for taking advantage of me. I had to come to terms with the fact that it just was not meant to be. The important thing about the breakup was that now I was able to see the poison I was feeding myself. My personal and professional growth allowed me to see the breakup as a blessing.

LOVE YOURSELF

I now know that because of how dysfunctional my upbringing was, it was not love and the promise of a bright and happy future I was holding onto, but a clinging and attachment to the abusive nature that was the foundation of the relationship.

I could not make her apologize or make her feel sorry for the things she put me through. But I can apologize to myself and make sure to never put myself in these kinds of positions where the love I have for someone else outweighs the love I have for myself. I have made mistakes. I should have left once I had the desire to cheat. Because of this, I formed principles to live by defining what love is for me as a man.

Principles of love

A man who says a woman will never understand how he can be in love and still cheat does not know what true love is. Love does not justify its actions with matters of the flesh, for love is not ignorance. Love is not breaking a woman's heart repeatedly, for love is not hurt. Love is not pain. Love does not surprise you with infidelity, for love is not deceit. Love is not selfish.

Love does not creep in the bed in the middle of the night or knock at your door with a secret love affair. There is no password or anything to hide with love. Love is not condescending. Love does not suffer from inferiority complexes, but of equality. For love is whole.

Love is not sleeping around with your child's co-creator or anyone for that matter and still try to claim your love rests solely with your significant other, because it is obvious that they are not significant at all. For love is honor. Love is respect, discipline. Love is self-control. You do not risk a lifetime of love and happiness for a moment of pleasure, that is not love.

Love is pure, authentic, and honest and to the point. If you are not ready to commit your all then be honest. Settling down is not something you figure out mentally, but a certainty you feel in your heart and soul to be faithful and committed not just to your loved one, but to yourself. You must love yourself enough, to love.

LOVE YOURSELF

To truly be in love, there must be that excitement. For love is joy, ambition, enlightenment. Love is hunger. That thirsty thought quenched by desires, knowing that she is the first thing on your mind in the morning and the last thing on your mind at night. Love is security, love is sacrifice. Love is confidence in a bond. Love is bragging rights. Love is confirmation.

Love is knowing what needs to be done and fixing it. Love is surviving storms. Love is withstanding. Love is deeper than it is suggested, for many men lack a proper digestion of what true love is. Love is transparent. To love, not in word or theory, but in action. Love is patience and not confusion. If the fear of losing the one you claim you love does not outweigh the novelty of something different then love is not what you have.

For a man understands his power and responsibility and knows that breaking a woman down only continues the cycle of mental poison that rolls over to our little girls and boys. I want my children to recognize what true love is. But first, I must be an example. I must be love.

"To love is to recognize yourself in another."
– Eckhart Tolle

Chemistry and Compatibility

When it comes to love in relationships, there are two words most of us unknowingly confuse and that's "chemistry" and "compatibility." Let's be clear, you can have chemistry and be incompatible. And be intellectually compatible without any romantic chemistry; so, what is chemistry and what causes us to think it means long-term compatibility? Why do we try to turn moments that should have remained moments into lifetimes? I will attempt to define chemistry based on my experiences.

Chemistry is that special thing that draws two individuals together naturally without any real effort. A natural flow. You want to be around this person like they were a best friend. It feels like you have known this person all your life. They just get you. You enjoy each other's company. You can speak on the phone for hours because there is always something to talk about. You enjoy the same activities and it feels like time just flies by when you are together.

We all usually look at chemistry from a physically compatible standpoint. Which is a combination of lust, infatuation, and desire. Though a romantic connection takes time to grow, a hug or a touch from this person feels like nothing you may have experienced. You can feel how sex will be with just a graze.

Now this is where chemistry gets tricky. Because you could have a strong chemistry physically, but not be made for each other as life-partners.

The mistake we all make every so often is that we introduce sex too soon. Which can be a huge distraction causing us not to pay attention to the red flags being waved. Or we see the red flags being waved but choose not to address it with our principles and values and evaluate the best move and decision for ourselves, so we wave it off. Why? Because we are basing our compatibility as life-partners off physical chemistry.

Believe it or not, you become spiritually connected once sexual energy is exchanged and it is extremely hard, without proper discipline, to see the truth for what it is. You put yourself in emotional harm's way because you do not fully understand this person's mental and emotional state, trauma and/or drama that you are potentially about to connect yourself too.

Forming a bond and connection with your potential partner by doing activities that represent your personality, character, and genuine interest is imperative in the first few months because spending time with each other is the only true way to build genuine intimacy. Not through sex.

The key is to wait at least three months. Three months of consistent dating on a weekly / bi-weekly pattern will get you where you need to be when you are considering someone to be your partner. Another essential element that helps facilitate knowing if you two are life partners are your zodiac signs. Your zodiac reveals vital details about one's personality. Like two fire signs are more likely to be compatible than a fire and water sign.

In fact, fire signs are most compatible with other fire signs as well as air signs. Understanding one's zodiac is not for the purpose of judging anyone or their character. That is what we have actions for. But instead to gauge one's personality in comparison to your own. A person who is a homebody and does not like going out for adventure and travel is likely to be incompatible with someone who must have adventures in their life.

You just mesh better with your element. A water and fire sign do not mix most of the time because of their contrast in personalities. Fire signs are gregarious extroverts with high energy and enthusiasm. Whereas water signs are more reserved introverts and like to keep their output of energy low. Too much fire will cause water to evaporate, just like too much water can drown out a fire.

This was the problem I shared in my last relationship. It was in the writing the whole time; the red flags were there regarding our personalities clashing but we chose to keep pushing with the relationship. Our spiritual bond was strong. For me personally, I could not leave that ass alone. She had a body to kill for. A mistake most men make.

I learned quickly that some things just need to be left alone. Two people should not have to work hard at trying to like one another. That is supposed to be the reason you are with that person.

Here are some things I noticed post relationship that I should have not ignored beforehand, as well as how to recognize the signs of mental abuse.

1. **Cannot be yourself**—If who you are as a person annoys your companion then it should be obvious that you are incompatible. In situations like this, working to be what they want you to be to give them peace, is not only draining, but makes you miserable. Your energy is important. If you cannot be yourself, how can you ever be happy? How do you spend so much time thinking about how not to be you, just to make

someone else happy? I noticed this early, but I waited too late. I waited until it started to affect our chemistry and by then it was too late.

2. **Lack of respect**—If they are calling you a loser. Saying you're stupid and just constantly putting you down, shaming you, if they have no interest in what interests you, always talking about your errors and failures in life just to make themselves feel better, not only do they have low self-esteem, but they have completely no respect for you at all and they are trying to break you down. And once they do not respect you the race is over. Lack of respect eats at your chemistry and removes the passion and affection. Once removed, the sex becomes cold, cheating begins, and now you really in and ain't shit.

3. **Blaming you for their problems**—One year my ex forgot my birthday and said it was my fault because I did not make any insinuations. Yes, you read correctly. It was my fault she forgot my birthday because I did not give her any clues. Most would say lack of accountability is issues that both sexes struggle with, but I hear from a lot of men that their main issue with the women they date is their inability to just admit they fucked up. If you cannot laugh at yourself when you screw up and admit when you are wrong, then you have insecurity issues and need to search for the root cause of why you are like that. Because if you do not solve that problem, you will only carry these and all your unresolved issues into your next relationship.

SIDENOTE: People do not understand that if they go into a new relationship or even a marriage with unhealed hurts, unresolved issues from their past, and a lack of understanding of who they really are as individuals, those hurts and issues do not just disappear with the novelty of new relationship or that marriage. Getting married is just a short-lived distraction from true reality. Once those feelings of superficial love and excitement disappear (as it does) and day-to-day life/interaction faces them, love will not be enough. So, get your shit together please.

4. **Teamwork**—If you are not willing to work together, whether that be exercising, watching documentaries and learning together, making money together, effectively communicating wants, needs and desires, then the relationship will be stale. You will get tired of one another because the relationship is not going anywhere. You must produce a system that works best for you that is not going to cause any toxic emotional disputes and that continuously grows your bond. You are supposed to build each other up. Be each other's high when one of you is low. Most importantly, you must listen to each other and value each other's opinion. Listening is the foundation of teamwork and the glue that keeps the love strong.

Mental abuse is one of the hardest forms of abuse to recognize. It wears down on your self-esteem making you feel bad about yourself. It makes you doubt yourself. It creates negative self-talk and grows nasty habits that will only keep you from being the best version of yourself. How people treat you reflects their own pain and suffering; it is not a reflection of who you are. Remove yourself immediately.

THE F.I.G TREE

What was your fear of losing that made you ignore all the red flags, specifically, that fact that you could not be you?
JAMAI: Honestly, her body. Big boobs, big ass, and a beautiful smile. I was willing to be miserable just so I could continue the lust and infatuation that I had for her.

What has your mate made you feel insecure about in your relationship? (Current or Past)
JAMAI: For not being where she felt a man of my age should be in life. She felt that I manipulated her into thinking I was this stable businessperson impenetrable to challenging times and financial instability when we first met because I had money. She viewed my depression during the pandemic as my being lazy and having a lack of effort. Which made me feel insecure as a man in whole. She was the only woman besides my mother who made me tear up about who I felt I was and my struggles as an entrepreneur, as a man, and a father.

What do you regret the most about your relationship? (Current or Past)
JAMAI: I "regret avoiding conflict to keep peace not knowing I was starting a war inside." And that is from a quote by Cheryl

Richardson. I did not check her or put her in her place when I should have. I was not firm and assertive enough. My being too understanding, too tolerable, and too respectful because she was young, inexperienced, and ignorant to things backfired because I created a culture that allowed her to express herself in a disrespectful manner. I gave her passes and let behaviors slide on things I did not know would emasculate me later.

THE F.I.G TREE

What was your *FEAR* of losing that made you ignore all the red flags?

_____

_____

_____

_____

What has your mate made you feel *INSECURE* about in your relationship? (Current or Past)

_____

_____

_____

_____

What do you *REGRET* the most about your relationship? (Current or Past)

_____

_____

_____

_____

I want you to write down the things you are looking for in a significant other. What are your requirements? You can get into brief details if you like. What kind of personality traits do you want them to have? Achievements? Character? Standards and Values? Wants, needs and desires?

_____

_____

_____

_____

_____

_____

_____

_____

LOVE YOURSELF

Ask yourself, do you meet the requirements of your requirements, yes or no?

_____

_____

_____

_____

Universal Laws

THE LAW OF REFLECTION.

> *"The Universal Law of Reflection states that we see the traits in others that exist in ourselves. The things that you love and admire in others are things that exist within you. Likewise, the things that you resist or find unpleasant in others, are things that exist within you.*
>
> *The world is just a mirror for you."*
>
> — Author Unknown

Good or bad, every situation that you are in and relationship that you have with others, whether romantically, platonic or business, will always be the direct reflection of the relationship that you have with yourself. I hope this reading experience has helped you in a way that gives you clarity, information, and inspiration, to fully understand yourself on your journey of personal growth. I am proud of you for taking the first step. Keep being dope and remember…it all begins with you.

Recap and Clarity

PT. 1—THE ROOT: UNDERSTANDING YOURSELF

From part one, you should have obtained the knowledge and understanding of where you learned love. You should have thought back to the very first time you fell in love as an adult. Analyzed and compared how that person loved you or the person who is loving you now, to the love you received from home or lack of. Some, if any emotional and verbal abuses that you may have experienced or are experiencing now that resembles what you received growing up.

You should have learned and understood how toxic behavior before proper healing only cuts and scars those who do not deserve to bleed. How important moving on from pain is. You should have made a connection to the results you received in your prior and/or recent relationship, from what you were conditioned with as a youth. You should be preparing to work on reprogramming habits and behavior so you do not make the same mistakes.

You have written down what you fear, what you are insecure about, and something you feel guilty about. Your goal is to use the Universal Law of Belief to conquer fear, the Universal Law of

Detachment to heal your insecurities, and the Universal Law of Forgiveness to forgive others and yourself for whatever personal guilt you hold on to.

Part 1 urges you to look at your childhood from the root of your trauma to understand why you are the way you are. If your belief is not stronger than your fear, if you do not want to prove to yourself through love instead of wanting to prove others wrong through anger, if forgiveness is not a part of your presence and you do not forgive the wrongs and letdowns of others and of yourself understanding that we all have our issues, your past will continue to cast any doubt, shame, and guilt over your future because you refuse to lift the weight. Applied and implemented, these three laws are what allow you to execute the next three laws in Part 2.

PT. 2—THE TRUNK: LOVING YOURSELF

In Part 2 I had you focus on things about your childhood you were good at. Any talents and passions that you left behind and could monetize today. You learned the difference between talent and passion. How to find what you are passionate about.

LOVE YOURSELF

How do you feel about life? You should understand that your happiness is your tab to pay. That your success or lack thereof begins with you. You should understand the power of mentorship. How important it is to get your shit together first.

You learned the importance of focusing on purpose before a relationship. To love yourself like you would love your significant other. That self-awareness is imperative in all relationships and the determining factor of winning and losing. You learned that your ego would do anything to protect itself from embarrassment. You should understand the power and contagion of confidence. That people believe what you believe. How wanting something is the seed to finding interest and passion. That every opportunity is not always the best. Learning how to say no. Putting yourself first. How selling yourself is more about the emotion than the product. To sell the solution. That you are your brand. The power of self-talk and visualization. What fear is and how to use it as motivation. And to keep dreaming no matter if it breaks your heart because dreams lead to purpose.

You should have written down, based on what you **Fear** the most, what you allow to distract you. Based on what you are **Insecure** about, why do you think you continue to allow these distractions to suffocate your focus? And what do you feel **Guilty** about? Your goal is to use the Universal Law of Intention to suffocate distractions, the Universal Law of Action to rid procrastination, and the Universal Law of Manifestation to focus your creativity and create your reality. Remember, **"you are a living magnet. What you attract into your life is in harmony with your dominant thoughts."** You manifest what you feel, not what you think.

Part 2 urges you to focus on your gifts and talents and how to monetize what you're naturally good at. These three laws are what allow your frequency to vibrate at its highest vibration. What you attract in your life is beneficial and desirable. Which is our next law, the Law of Attraction.

PT. 3—THE BRANCHES: YOUR AWAKENING

Part 3 begins with being aware of the signs communicating with you. These signs are letting you know you are on the right path and to continue to do what you are doing. When you are walking your purpose and doing what makes you happy you drip in authenticity. It is felt when you speak. People want to work with you. They want to help you and be a part of what you do. Which is why the universal law here is attraction. The more in tune you are, the stronger your magnet becomes. This makes all your interactions prosperous.

LOVE YOURSELF

PT. 4—THE LEAVES: LOVING AGAIN

You should have come to terms with the truth of your reality. Forgiven yourself. Respect yourself. Let go of the weight and are ready to flourish. Creating boundaries and principles for yourself to protect your integrity.

You should understand that everything both good and bad in your relationship is what is good and bad with the relationship you have with yourself. That everything is a direct reflection of you. Which is why you must meet your own requirements.

Part 4 urges you to understand that you are the root source of the problems you are having. Fix yourself and be willing to fight and work on things within the relationship as well. I do not agree that you must necessarily come into a relationship with everything in check, we are humans. But you must be willing to work hard on whatever needs to be worked on if it is worth it.

You should have written down what you are most afraid of regarding love. What you are most insecure about with your mate (current or past). And what you regret the most about your relationship. If you are a man in a relationship and you have answered these questions truthfully you learned two things:

It's either time to give it up or if the love is genuine, reevaluate your relationship and begin from nothing. Second, never let any woman cut your balls off because you want to be Mr. Understanding. Demand respect always. Everything is a reflection on how you treat and love yourself. Be masculine. If you allow her to get away with acts of non-love and disrespect, then what does that say about how you feel about yourself?

Ladies, never let any man make you feel like you cannot do better. He should not be disrespecting you. Stop allowing men to get away with things that prove they do not respect you. Stand up for yourself. If you are a young lady or man and have not experienced love yet, then you know exactly what to avoid and the perspective to have. Take it one day at a time and keep pushing. I love you.

Acknowledgements

First, I would like to thank my beautiful, sweet cousin, Kionna Wray. The success I have achieved as an entrepreneur and educator is due in part to her linking me with Mr. Kevin Allen, her godfather. Thank you for the direction cuzzo, I am where I am because of you.

To my now mentor and friend, Mr. Kevin Allen, the man who is responsible for introducing me to the former Principal and current Congressman, Dr. Jamaal Bowman. When I put my first book in this man's hand, he said… "If I like it, I'm going to change your life." The rest is history.

And finally, Congressman Jamaal Bowman, who I cannot thank enough. He resuscitated my life when I was lost. I did not know what I had with my first book nor did I understand my value. I did not understand the power of sharing your story until I met him, he gave me the perspective I needed. In his school was where, for the first time, I shared my story. In his school is where my purpose was chiseled and defined. It was in his school where I worked and built what I have now. There will be no story of triumph without having him in my life. Thank you, Sir, and thank you all.

Always grateful,
Jamai Wray

"In you, you should trust."

About the Author

Jamai Wray is a writer, educational consultant, curriculum developer, and contracted vendor for the New York City Department of Education. He is the author of *The Random Thoughts Lifebook: A Personal and Social Awareness, Life and Entrepreneurial Skills* workbook, which has been taught in middle and high schools in the greater New York area. His first book, *The Random Thoughts of a Philosophy Major-Drop: The Philosophy of My Life*, has sold over 100,000 units and is the book he says saved his life. Jamai has been a lifelong writer who got his start writing music. His joy and love for his craft is stated in his quote, "I have the best job because I get to be the person I wish I had growing up."

Also by Jamai Wray

The Random Thoughts of a Philosophy Major Drop-Out: The Philosophy of My Life. Published. 2013.
ISBN: 978-0-578-62696-3

The Random Thoughts Lifebook: A Personal and Social Awareness Life and Entrepreneurial Skills workbook. (For 8th—12th graders & young adults) Published. 2016
ISBN: 978-0-578-60175-5
Website www.mwrayent.com www.jamaiwray.com

HANDLES

- IG:@jamaiwray FB: Jamai Wray
- Tik: @jamaiwray
- LinkedIn: Jamai Wray
- Email: mwrayent@gmail.com

Selected Bibliography

Deida, David. *The Way of the Superior Man.* Boulder, CO: Sounds True Publishers, 1997, 2004, 2017. Quote.

Greene, Robert and Jackson, Curtis. *The 50th law.* New York, NY: HarperCollins Publishers, 2009.

Sicinski, Adam. *The Universal Law of belief and its impact on your life.* Blog IQ Matrix. http://blog.iqmatrix.com

Wong, Kenneth. *The Millennial Grind.* Blog. https://millennial-grind.com/20-quotes-on-the-law-of-detachment/ (Quote by Deepak Chopra)

Butler, Amanda. *The Universal Law of forgiveness.* SelfGrowth.com. http://www.selfgrowth.com/articles/The_Universal_Law_of_Forgiveness.html

Deida, David. *The Way of the Superior Man.* Boulder, CO: Sounds True Publishers, 1997, 2004, 2017. Quote.

Jones, Derrick T, Nichols, Allan G, Kaylan, Howard, Barbara, Johnny, Volman, Mark R and James, William. *My name is D-Nice.* New York, NY: Universal Music Publishing Group.

Hillman, James. *The force of character.* New York, NY: Random House, 1999.

Walmsley, Joanne. *Numerology/Angel Numbers.* The Sacred Scribes BlogSpot. http://sacredscribesangelnumbers.blogspot.com/search?q=1127 http://sacredscribesangelnumbers.blogspot.com/search?q=911 http://sacredscribesangelnumbers.blogspot.com/

search?q=156 http://sacredscribeangelnumbers.blogspot.com/search?q=444

Psychic Elements Author - Psychic Elements Staff. *The Universal Law of Inspired Action.* How to use Universal Laws to create your perfect life. October 3, 2017. https://psychicelements.com/blog/how-to-use- universal-laws-to-create-your-perfect-life

www.ingramcontent.com/pod-product-compliance
Lightning Source LLC
Chambersburg PA
CBHW041139110526
44590CB00027B/4072